SPEECH AND LANGUAGE DEVELOPMENT OF THE PRESCHOOL CHILD

SPEECH AND LANGUAGE DEVELOPMENT OF THE PRESCHOOL CHILD

A Survey

By

COLLEEN WILKINSON McELROY, M.A.

Assistant Professor of Speech Therapy
Supervisor of Clinical Services
Western Washington State College
Bellingham, Washington

With a Foreword by

Thomas Billings, Ph.D.

Professor of Education
Western Washington State College
Bellingham, Washington

CHARLES C THOMAS • PUBLISHER

Springfield • Illinois • U.S.A.

Published and Distributed Throughout the World by
CHARLES C THOMAS • PUBLISHER
BANNERSTONE HOUSE
301-327 East Lawrence Avenue, Springfield, Illinois, U.S.A.
NATCHEZ PLANTATION HOUSE
735 North Atlantic Boulevard, Fort Lauderdale, Florida, U.S.A.

ISBN 0-398-02368-9
Library of Congress Catalog Card Number: 75-184604

Printed in the United States of America
PP-22

For David

THE DOLL BELIEVERS

This lifeless construction,
Yellow hair curled and twisted,
The forever motionless face of rubber,
The dark marked eyebrows,
The pug nose of flexible material,
Spongy cheeks painted red,
Camel-hair eyebrows moving up and down.
Lifting her up, the eyes fly open,
They stare into space unmoved,
Those deep blue and soft eyes,
Those never winking, moving balls,
Controlled from the inside,
And that thick rubber body,
The imprint of a navel,
The undersized hands,
The thick soft knees,
The screwed-on head,
The air hole behind her neck,
All this in its lifelessness
Gives me a feeling that children
Are really powerful people
To imagine that such a thing
Could be alive.

FOREWORD

THERE are three reasons for my accepting an invitation to prepare a foreword for this remarkably interesting and competent book, *Speech and Language Development of the Preschool Child*. First, the book is concerned with the oldest, most intimate, and by any measure, one of the most mysterious of human invention, namely, human language. Although the book does not pretend to philosophical or philological depth, it does raise hard practical questions that will, if confronted seriously, force the student of language and speech into weighty and critical philosophic matters. The book will compel him to confront old, durable "open questions" like, Do we think better because we use the right words, or do we use the right words because we think better? Or, when a child learns a language, what is it that he has learned? The easy answer is that he has learned the *meanings* of the words and sentences of the language. If this answer is to be useful, we must decide what a *meaning* is and how we know when a person has learned one.

This book should encourage serious students of speech and language to reread classical inquiries into the nature of language and personality like those conducted by Edward Sapir, Benjamin Lee Whorf, Frederick Nietzsche, Lewis Carroll, George Miller, and Charlton Laird.

The book should also alert students to new dimensions of humor in the sardonic observation: Isn't it curious that when God wanted to become an author he studied Greek, and that poorly.

A second reason for writing this introduction is that the book addresses itself to an acutely practical problem of language and dialect which, unless solved, threatens to widen the distance and increase the hatreds between the numerous and varied language and dialect communities which make up the nation. As the former director of a national education program for *economically* disadvantaged youth, many of whom were members of linguistically different cultures, I know how common and how devastating it is to equate economic disadvantage with cultural and linguistic inadequacy and inferiority. Indeed, the equation often implies moral bankruptcy as well! The language of the ghetto, the barrio, the "holler" and the reservation is often as complete, as profound, and as subtle as the language of the classroom and the cocktail lounge, and it is always more earthy and colorful! Whatever else it is, it is a particular community's inventory of reality, a unique code with and within which the members of the community structure their perceptions and experiences. The language code is the stuff of which *minds* are made; tamper with the code and you have, at the same time, tampered with the minds of those whose code it is. As Sapir argues, "Language is not merely a more or less systematic inventory of the various items of experience which seem relevant to the individual, as is so often naively assumed, but is also a self-contained, creative symbolic organization, which not only refers to experience largely acquired without its help but actually defines experience for us by reason of its formal completeness and because of our unconscious projection of its implicit expectations into the field of experience."

The chapters of this book devoted to shedding new light on this issue are as valuable as any I have read. Had these insights been available ten years ago to those who work with culturally and dialectically different youngsters, perhaps some of the subtle tragedies of the ominous decade just passed might have been mitigated or avoided altogether.

A final reason for this introduction is that it gave me an opportunity to read and recommend the work of a colleague whose interests and training are clinical and practical whereas mine have been largely philosophic and speculative. The profession to which we are both committed has suffered through time by separating its philosophic and speculative from its practical and clinical functions. The two realms, theory and practice, are as inextricably bound as thought is to its expression, as bound as ideas are to the words within which they are formulated and expressed. The relationship between "language," "thought," and "reality" is intimate and deep. This book is about these intimate and critical relationships.

An extensive clinical experience and formidable powers of analysis and synthesis have permitted the author to write this remarkably significant book.

Thomas Billings

PREFACE

THE world of the child continues to be the most fascinating aspect of human existence. A great deal of that fascination lies in the mystery of the child's world. Once the child becomes an adult, he loses insight to the mystery of childhood. Never again will he be able to gain so much knowledge and develop so many complex and varied skills in such a short period of time. The adult cannot rid himself of all problems, large and small, and totally enjoy the very act of enjoying as he did as a child. This fascination with the child's world has led modern research to ask many questions: What does the child *really* think? What does he *really* see? Moreover, the field of education has become concerned with, What does he *really* enjoy? Innovative (and controversial) education says "Learning can be fun," and they mean for children as well as for teachers. Before we can rid ourselves of the "joyless" classrooms, we must somehow understand the world of the child.

This book is designed to explore that world, particularly the language of the child. This is not a text for advanced research, but an introductory text to the great mystery of language acquisition and development. It is my intention to survey the *areas* of language development so that the beginning student can obtain a breadth of knowledge regarding this subject.

Language acquisition and development has, for the most part, been discussed as a "pure" phenomenon. Yet the child does not develop language in a vacuum. This book will, then, attempt to relate other areas of maturation and the environment to the area of language. It should serve as a suitable reference for beginning students in psychology, education, speech pathology, and sociology. It is the author's fond wish that it might also serve as a reference for anyone interested in child language, including parents. Indeed, much of what is discussed in this book is in response to questions most commonly asked by parents. It is for these reasons that much of the text involves only an explanatory mention of specific research data and statistical information. It is also the reason for refraining from the use of complex terminology commonly found in advance research texts. To be sure, terminology is used; however, considerable care was taken to choose those terms most commonly utilized in the various fields of research.

Perhaps, like any survey text, this one suffers from the effects of a cursory view in many areas. With all due apologies to the ardent researchers and philosophers of those fields, a cursory view is intended. The subject of each chapter could stand alone as a text and, in many instances, has served as subject matter for various books. This, however, is the very reason for a survey. The beginning student in any field finds it difficut to coalesce information from a great number of sources. Psycholinguistics can perhaps boast of the greatest number of late entries to specific area texts. Psychology and child development sources are numerous and well-read. Sources on speech disorders and innovative education grow in number. Mass communication texts cover a wide variety of interests. More recently, the "disadvantaged" child has come under close scrutiny as well. All of these are available to those students who may seek a specialty. Many of these sources are included in the bibliography of this book. There are, however, a limited number of books that attempt to include all areas of maturation and development.

In order to orient the student to the field of language acquisition and development, Chapter One of this text, "Historical Perspective," will be concerned with the students' attitude toward language and how this attitude may interfere with his objective study of language development. It will discuss those factors that might hamper the study of language, such as cultural impress, attitudinal sets, and by the very nature of the subject—the complexity of language. It will also take a very brief look at the various theories of language origin in Man.

Chapter Two "Language Acquisition—Learned Versus Innate," begins the discussion of child language. This chapter is a general discussion of how the child acquires language. Basic theoretical views on language acquisition in children are discussed. Performance, auditorization, memory, and intelligence are defined as the basic requirements for language development. Chapter Two does not solve the question of acquisition but it does offer a number of basic approaches to prelinguistic requirements.

Chapter Three differentiates speech and language. Speech is defined as the tool of language; while language is defined as the function of communication. Speech and language are divided into four basic factors. Developmental theories are reintroduced and competence versus performance is discussed. This chapter serves as a way of defining and identifying the phenomenon that will be "tracked" in the following chapter.

Chapter Four, "Neurophysiological Development," is an overview of the neurological mechanism necessary for speech and language development. Motorical stages of development are also presented. The development of the neurological process for speech will be described and the pathways utilized in that process will be illustrated through the use of schematas.

Chapter Five, "Language and Cognition," will trace the expansion of sensory information from the beginning stages when the child is motivated by tactile sensations to later stages when he is primarily visually oriented. It will relate sensory information to linguistic development and the thinking process.

Psychosocial perception is the subject of Chapter Six. Social maturity as it relates to the child's physical need for independence is explored in this chapter. Social maturity is related to the initial dependence on perceptual coding to the stage of independence and conceptual coding. The child's use of time-space-casual relationships in the development of conceptual coding is discussed.

Chapter Seven, "Dialect: Considerations of Difference," involves the consideration of language difference. It is included in this text as a "normal" process. The relationship of cultural values and language development are explored. The historical implications of research involving dialect and language differences as well as the importance of studying bidialectal "switching" and bilingual "translation" activities are considered.

Chapter Eight, "Evaluation of Language Development," considers test procedures and test instruments. The elusiveness of that human element, "intelligence," is considered. Examples of various tests that might be used in a comprehensive evaluation of language development are presented.

Chapter Nine, "The Child from Birth to Age Five," describes the child as a communicator and is discussed in terms of his responsibilities in the role of listener and the role of speaker at various stages of development. Normative data for the previously considered areas of development are related. Examples of language behavior are provided for illustrative purposes.

A definite attempt has been made in this book to relate all of the various aspects of development to the area of language. I have been particularly careful to include language difference as one of those aspects. Throughout the book, the student is cautioned against a priori assumptions regarding language effectiveness. The "grammarian" approach has been avoided as well as value judgment of "good and bad" language. If there is an ultimate purpose to this book, it is that *all* children can be viewed as "powerful people" who, in spite of the efforts of adults, develop the greatest tool of all—language.

COLLEEN W. MCELROY

ACKNOWLEDGMENTS

FOR those friends and colleagues of mine who shared my views and who were available for support when I needed it, I wish to extend my sincere appreciation. I am particularly grateful to Margaret Jacobs, Maile Pringle, Erhart Schinske, Ellen Burdick, Beverly Hanna, and Loren Webb for their assistance. A special thanks to those friends who "loaned" me their children: Mr. and Mrs. Peter Smith, Mr. and Mrs. Reg Butler, Mr. and Mrs. Walter Charbonneau, Mr. and Mrs. Tom Heidlebaugh, and Mr. and Mrs. Jerry Bailey. I am grateful to all of those who permitted me to quote from their publications and to the faculty of Western Washington State College and the Bureau for Faculty Research.

I would also like to thank the many students of Western Washington State College who encouraged me to "screw myself to the sticking place" and write this book. It is through their many promptings that this text has developed. To Joan Camper, artist, and Rollin Wood, photographer, I extend a most humble thanks. I would like to honor my family for their patience and thank them for their help.

Finally, I am indebted to my husband for his encouragement and invaluable assistance.

C. W. M.

CONTENTS

209

SPEECH AND LANGUAGE DEVELOPMENT OF THE PRESCHOOL CHILD

Chapter One

HISTORICAL PERSPECTIVE

SPEECH is man's most unique function. It separates him from the rest of the animal kingdom and makes him more than just the *Naked Ape* that Desmond Morris would have us believe he is. It is one of the tools that helps him develop all those worldly and materialistic goods that make him a universal rather than a regional creature. Although he is, historically, a tribal and familial creature, speech makes him a "brother" (not necessarily ethnic, political or spiritual) to all mankind. It is the common denominator that carries man beyond the natural boundaries of time and space. The implications of that statement are realized in the Arabic quotation: "Language is the steed that carries one into a far country." and further reflected in another by a long forgotten philosopher: "The limits of my language mean the limits of my world."

EARLY THEORIES

Most researchers will agree that speech begins in much the same way in every living child, but none can agree on the origins of speech in the species of man. Some clues to the mystery of the origin of language are provided by relying on proverbs or quotes. Pei (1965), for example, quotes Hawthorne as saying that "language—human language, after all, is but little better than the croak and crackle of fowls and other utterances of brute nature—sometimes not so adequate." One of the earliest recorded studies of language occurred in 610 B.C. Since then, written theories about language have not been wanting. Some are traditional and mystic. Most are confusing. In the seventeenth century, a Swedish researcher stated that in the Garden of Eden, God spoke Swedish, Adam Danish, and the serpent French (Pei, 1956).

Language theories span the ridiculous to the sublime. There

is a theory called the "bow-wow" theory. Then there are the "pooh-pooh" and "ding-dong" theories (Pei, 1965; Brown, 1958; Grey and Wise, 1946), and still another that this author refers to as the "ethereal" theory. The bow-wow theory holds that language arose in imitation of the sounds occurring in nature; that language is onomatopoetic. The trouble with this is that the same natural noise is heard differently by different people. If man were just imitating natural noises, he would have a universal language, not a cock-a-doodle for English chickens and chic-chirichi for Italian ones. The pooh-pooh theory states that language first consisted of primitive inarticulate chants to denote surprise, fear, pain, pleasure, and so forth (some of which is still contained in all languages).

The ding-dong theory enters another area in that it maintains that there is a mystic correlation between sound and meaning. This hypothesis states that man, when struck by the nature of things, "rings" or speaks instinctively. This is generally discarded in serious scientific discussion since the correlation cannot be easily demonstrated. The "yo-he-ho" theory states that language arose as a result of grunts produced by physical exertion. It, too, is generally disregarded by modern researchers. The ethereal theory is very much like the ding-dong, only perhaps more biblical. It is of the *2001 Space Odyssey* category in which the appearance of a monolith changed the course of history taking us from the level of the ape to the level of man. In this theory, some sort of sign also changed the course of man producing him as we have him today—verbal beyond belief.

DISTINCTION BETWEEN SPEECH AND LANGUAGE

These are only a few examples of theories of language origins. They do, however, clarify one aspect of this phenomena; that is, that language is a composite of sounds, some intelligible and some not, and that languages are at least universal in their origin and function. Notice that I have not used interchangeably the terms speech and language. It is imperative that the student of language acquisition recognize the difference. Ferdinand de Saussare was one of the first theorists to attempt to make a distinction between the act of language and what constituted that act (Lyons,

1969). De Saussure used the terms *langue* and *parole. Langue* was designated as that which is shared by speakers of a common language. Speakers of English, therefore, share a particular *langue* common only to English. *Parole* was a term used to designate the set of utterances produced when speaking a language. *Langue* is common to all speakers of English, but only when they are in the act of speaking, uttering, do they exhibit instances of *parole.* De Saussure set up this distinction to emphasize the complex relationship between the utterance and the realization of those utterances (units of *langue* or sentences). Using this as a basic formula, we can make the distinction between speech and language *Parole is* the tool, the speech portion of language. *Langue* is the function, the language portion of speaking.

Consider that speech is the utterance of sounds, while spoken language is the transmission of those utterances to another individual in an intelligible and meaningful fashion. Speech is the production of sounds first reflexively, then repetitively, and finally, learned. In other words, the child first produces sounds that are not propositional. Berry and Eisenson (1956) define propositional speech as meaningful units of speech which are of communicative value. Initial sound production is a by-product of feeding behavior, crying behavior, and coincidental vocalization during generalized activity. When the child begins to control his vocalizations, he repeats some of these same sounds intentionally. Finally, he begins to correct his production in accordance with environmental stimulation and reinforcement. Speech sound production has become a developed skill. This process will be further explained in Chapter Two.

When the child begins to use these speech sounds to transfer ideas and to relate to the environment, he has begun to use language or propositional speech. He symbolizes (translates) ideas into concepts. Let us examine that last statement. First of all, he symbolizes—he develops words for objects, people, or actions. This does not mean that he is able to automatically use those words to express his needs. For example, a college student may recognize a word used in a text book without actually being able to use that word in a functional manner. Think of the word "quondam." It may be familiar but not what you would call the ordinary "run-of-the-mill" word. Children are faced with a similar situation early in their speech careers. If they have the word, they are able to symbolize. If they can use the word functionally, they are able to conceptualize.

Search for Self

Perhaps this process appears fairly simple if viewed in this "cut and dried" manner. It is, however, a complex process and, by its very nature, this complexity hampers our ability to view language in an objective manner. There are many factors that hamer our view of language. One of the factors most often ignored is that language is a search for self. This is particularly important to remember in the study of the child's language. It has been said that without language a child remains a child. He cannot offer or share ideas. He cannot experiment, change, or justify his actions. It is essential to remember that any study of language development must consider that the child's view of the world is quite different from that of the adult's and that a child's behavior is an expression of his search for self. His self-image influences reception and transmission of signals because of the constantly moving and changing patterns of the world. It is essential then to understand the child's world.

The child's world is limited, first of all by size. He is simply not physically equipped to handle the adult world. Secondly, it is limited by experience. He cannot anticipate events and his emotions are not controlled by social restrictions. Finally, it is limited by the environment. He is not independent and can function only within the world of the adults that surround him. These limitations are exemplified in the following story:

> There was a little boy who was hospitalized to have his tonsils removed. He was about four or five years old. He was placed in a hospital in which there was a central nurses's station for each section of the ward. Each station was equipped with a talk-back televiewing system so that the nurse could check on the patients without ever leaving the station. During the first night of his hospitalization prior to the operation, a nurse checked his room to see if he was all right. The television camera "homed" in on the bed and could not find the little boy, so the nurse called the little boy over the audio system. "Tommy, Tommy, are you there? Are you all right?" There

> was no answer. She called several times. "Tommy, Tommy, are you there?" and at the same time, checked the room with the camera to see if she could find him. There was no sign of him. Finally, after a long while a little voice answered in the corner, "What do you want, Wall?"

This story, aside from its obvious humor, illustrates how anything is possible in a child's world. A child lives in a wonderland where chairs can talk, animals wear clothes, and walls can talk.

Speech and Speaker

Another aspect of language that hampers our study of this complex phenomena is that *we are prone to remove speech from the speaker.* The more abstract we become about language, the less we know about it. This has been true of most of the early language theories previously described. All of these theories are examples of how hard we try to analyze language by analyzing the utterances or sounds that man produces without considering the man, as if these utterances were "crystallized essence of man." Here is a story that will illustrate the futility of this type of research:

> There was an explorer who "stumbled" upon what came to be considered a long, lost tribe. In the course of discovering all there was to know about this tribe, a linguist was sent to transcribe their language system. When he arrived on the scene, no member of the tribe would talk to him for many days. Finally, one stray, lonely-looking member came up to him and began to converse. After a while, the linguist coaxed this tribe member to tape record names most commonly used by the tribe, ideas held sacred, etc., as well as many hours of conversation that were little more than gossip. Then the linguist winged his way back to the home university where he transcribed all of the recordings. To his surprise and the fascination of his colleagues, many of the sounds transcribed were repetitive. There were definite prolongations and hesitations and the researcher spoke of strange gestures that seemed to be incorporated into the patterns of speech. He wrote up his findings into a fine Ph.D. dissertation, and in due course it was published. Some years later, another linguist went to the same tribe. He discovered that the first linguist had talked to the only stutterer in the tribe who was an outcast and a notorious liar.

If we are to deal with communication, we must deal with the

speaker, his personality, his environment, and the listener. Language is not an isolated phenomenon. The process of symbolization (word development) is complex. As man developed a more complex culture, the signal system of communication became less effective. A signal system of communication is one in which immediate ideas are transferred by a rigid code. The complexity of man's existence was reflected in his symbolic behavior. The use of the term complex merely indicates that man progressed from the use of the simple, fixed signal system to the flexible, less finite symbolic system. Furth (1969) illustrates the difference between the two systems in the following schemata:

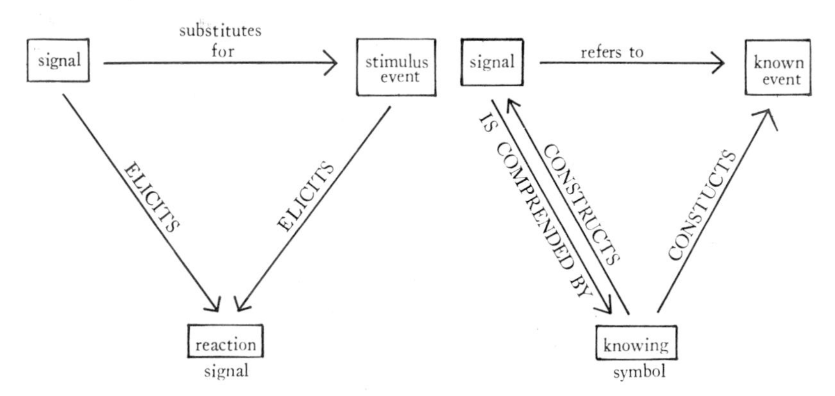

Figure 1. Sign relations: The difference between signs and symbols. (From Hans G. Furth, *Piaget and Knowledge: Theoretical Foundations,* © 1969. Reprinted by permission of Prentice-Hall, Englewood Cliffs, New Jersey.)

Signals are usually simple and commonly isolated. The orientation to a signal is temporal and environmental. Signals are time-bound and situational, whereas symbols are time-free with no limitations of time-space and person. Symbols are complex and systematized. In a signal, the meaning is referential and external. In a symbol, the meaning is assigned and internal.

In a signal system, for example, a green light means "go"; a red light means "stop"; the ringing of a bell means "attention." Animal language is a signal system. We certainly continue to use the signal system; however, we have embellished the system and made it much more complex. We have developed a verbal system.

When we rearranged the universe to a more "man-made" image, we also rearranged our language. For example, what do you think when you hear the following words?: think–bell, think–bread, think–computerized, think–democracy. Some of you will think "alarm" for the illustration "bell": getting up in the morning, returning from school. For "bread," some of you will think of a loaf of bread, a slice of bread, a jelly sandwich, bread and butter; any one of the concrete images associated with bread.

But what will happen for "computerized"? Some of you will see images of numbers. Others will see images of machines. "Democracy" will stimulate even more images—some concrete, others ambiguous. This leads us to believe that "democracy" is more involved or "abstract" than the concept "bread." Furth (1969) states that we behave toward signals by more or less automatic external movements, whereas symbols follow from or lead to an internal action of knowing. In other words, signs involve practical, external activity while symbols involve cognitive, internal activity.

As man gained more control over his environment, he developed words that would explain and preserve his behavior. There was a need for a symbolic system. Man is a verbal animal in a self-developed verbal world.

Attitudinal Sets

Another factor that often hampers our view of the language is that we tend to regard language *only in terms of our own associations with language.* We have developed certain attitudes about language. These reactions are often referred to as "attitudinal sets." An attitudinal set alters the response of any individual and also alters any linguistic unit received and delivered by the individual. When we read about ideas regarding language, we tend to relate to those ideas in terms that are most familiar to us. We will regard one type of phenomenon as strange and another type of phenomenon as familiar, based on our attitudes about phenomena and experiences with phenomena.

This is true, not only of the beginning student in language study, but also the linguist and psychologist. Earlier, researchers found it strange that Eskimos had no abstract units for such things as nuclear fission. On the other hand, they also found it strange that Eskimos had many words for snow. More recently, linguists have come to accept this as a peculiarity of the Eskimo language system. Professional researchers still find it strange, however, to accept verbal withdrawal as a means of communication. Yet, there is an Indian tribe in which the adult members considered the most learned are those members who are also the most nonverbal (Bunker, 1956).

Our preconceived fixed notions regarding language behavior tend to befuddle our thoughts about language systems other than our own. For example, Boas (in Hymes, 1964) states, ". . . primitive man when conversing is not in the habit of using abstractions." A more realistic statement would not refer to man as "primitive" based solely on his ability to use *abstractions*. The *Random House Dictionary* (Unabridged Edition) defines abstraction as: "an impractical idea; something visionary and unrealistic; the act of considering something as a general quality or characteristic, apart from concrete realities, specific objects, or actual instances."

Abstraction, then, does not imply technology but extracting the essence in a visionary manner, such as in religion or superstition. Primitive man was religious *and* superstitious (much like his modern brother). Perhaps Hymes is referring to "manner" of abstraction. It is not that primitive man did not abstract, but that he did not abstract in Western man's manner. This would seem plausible since the primitive world had a vastly different life style. Perhaps the terms *spoken system culture* can be substituted for primitive, while *recording system culture* can be used to designate the beginning of written information and a more technical society. It is obvious, of course, that this only serves to add to the confusion. We cannot develop a single term or phrase that will describe man's speech behavior over a period of time without describing the other changes that occurred during that period. To attempt to describe language patterns in some primitive–standard anthropological dicotomy is erroneous at any rate. Any number of studies (e.g. Chomsky, 1965; Lenneberg, 1964) have given evidence that "primitive" languages never existed. The ability to abstract must be present in order for any language to exist. The lack of sophisticated technology does not infer lack of complex language structure. All languages are equally complicated and have the qualities of abstraction. All written records of now-extinct languages, as well as all historical linguistic reconstructions of past linguistic forms, seem to be based on these same structuring principles (Houston, 1970).

Cultural Impress

Another factor that hampers our views of language is what I call "cultural impress." Any attempt to study both language and the culture must be timely. Today, it is imperative. The age-old thesis of cultural classification involves the ideas of primitive and civilized as well as correct and incorrect. In fact, it equates primitive with incorrect and civilized with correct. It is particularly important to view language realistically at this point in our history when polarization of cultures is both more evident and more devastating. To quote some researchers without explanation would be disastrous since the moralistic views of writers are often inherent in their work. McNeill (1966), for example, states that "The lower class child is retarded at least in part because he must work out the appropriate English manifestation of linguistic universals on his own. He must discover such features as noun and verb inflections from the haphazard stream of speech that happens to issue willy-nilly from his parents (p. 76)."

This kind of statement is classic and can be compared to the mistakes made in poverty programs when they insist that the children in those programs need lots of love (as if the children could not get it elsewhere, least of all from home). This is not to say that some of these children do not get love or that some of them are not consistently reinforced and stimulated in their speech efforts. The McNeill statement, however, would imply that upper class children are washed in an overabundance of love and are not subject to the same type of random reinforcement from their parents as are other children. High income and high IQ does no more to insure a child against ineffectual parents than low income and low IQ against effective ones.

Some research merely suggests or implies judgment. For example, research that generalizes about *all* Black dialects from a sample of children's speech carries many implications. The major implication is that the ghetto child can adequately represent the ghetto adult. Yet it would be difficult to imagine one adult of any section of the country admitting that the neighbor's six-year-old (or ten-year-old for that matter), represents the speech potential of the community. It would be preposterous to imagine any adult admitting that the six-year-old Vermont youngster represents the adult speech of the Hollywood community. Yet there have been studies that have generalized the adult speech of *the* ghetto from a child's conversation (Williams, 1970). There are also those statements that I prefer to call "manifestations of the intimacy of the ruling society." In other words, the meaning (semantics) of an utterance is not viewed as moralistic on the part of the ruling society since it never occurs to them to question the utterance. For example, "Is it true blondes have more fun?" is an assumption which anticipates that all people consider that merely by being blonde, you will have some degree of "fun." Substitute, "Is it true clubfeet have more fun" for your own clarification. We continue to read about Columbus' "discovery" of America as if the country had not been occupied prior to his arrival. If this view is acceptable, then it is clear why some of those same writers note that the first occupants (Indians), "roamed" (a term most often used to note animal movements) rather than travelled or migrated, as other men do. Clearly, our use of words to describe behavior and events is more than just a combination of sounds uttered at a particular moment.

In any study of language development, we must consider how we shape the language of the adult by imposing social restrictions on his communication patterns. This begins very early in life. The young child first discovers the limits of his world by "taste-testing" that world. He is tactually oriented. "Mother" is not a face, but hands and a warm body. He relates, not to the expression in the eyes, but to the feel of the hands, to the gentleness of touch. This tactual orientation does not stop when his point of focus travels to the floor. There he must also taste-test the environment. Sooner or later, however, we impose restrictions on his tactile orientation; there are things that you can touch and things you must never touch. These help the child develop attitudinal sets or value judgments about what is to be considered good, bad, or indifferent. In Western civilization, touch is not considered an essential part of communication. We rarely touch one another. Touch has become, in effect, taboo. We never touch a stranger and "excessive" touching is limited to the most intimate members of your family. There are societies, however, in which touch is considered an essential part of communication. Men are encouraged to hug one another and the conversation is not possible unless the people are in close physical contact. Church (1961) states that "We maintain a zone of sensitivity within which we tolerate intrusion only by those people with whom we want to be intimate; when two people stand talking, they stay a fairly constant distance apart and if one moves forward, the other immediately moves back."

The Arab and Balinese people, on the other hand, do not find touch nearly as disagreeable and conversations are held with a minimum of distance between the speakers. In recent years, we have begun to become concerned about our lack of sensitivity. A new corp of experts now agrees that what we need to do is return to the exploration of tactile sensations. There are some who would argue that the lack of communication between generations has been caused by this loss of tactual orientation within the family circle. In other words, we attempt to discuss the communication gap and, in the process of this discussion, we have "discovered" touch. It has become quite fashionable to write about the "new"' touch sensitivity. Yet this is the sensitivity that the child uses to verify his ideas about the environment and establish language.

Speaker and Listener

Another aspect of communication that hampers our view of language is *the role of the speaker and the listener*. A speech situation can never be duplicated once the speaker has uttered the first word. Each speech situation is different because the listener and speaker rarely react in the exact same fashion on two different occasions. Moreover, the speaker can rarely reduplicate the situation. We can never accurately reproduce the speech situation, for even as we view the situation on video tape recorders

The child's early life is focused on a tactile sense of trust and understanding. (Courtesy Wood Photographs)

and instant playbacks, we remember the original situation. Our memory of the initial situation alters response to the second situation. Speech sounds can never be duplicated because the same set of circumstances do not operate for any one set of sounds. When we attempt to duplicate a word, or a group of sounds, that duplication is based on our ability to remember the first utterance and also, on our ability to imitate the first utterance. Since I am not going to take the view of a phonetician in this book, I will not dwell on sound repetition.

The view here is that language is a combination of sounds used to transmit *ideas.* The form that these ideas will take depends upon many factors and not just the utterance of sounds. First of all, each speaking situation is different. The speaker relates to the authority figure, the parental figure, the child, with a different degree of interpretation altered by the immediate environment. His view of the environment and his ability to relate to the speaker depends on his physical and psychological state at the time of utterance. It is also altered by the social restrictions of the particular situation. Furthermore, he is restricted to respond within the boundaries of his sensory equipment, that is, on how well he perceives the clues of this particular speaking situation. Once he has uttered the idea, he uses feedback to check his communication skills. This is illustrated in the following schemata.

The listener in turn must go through the same check and recheck devices in order to respond to the utterance. The listener

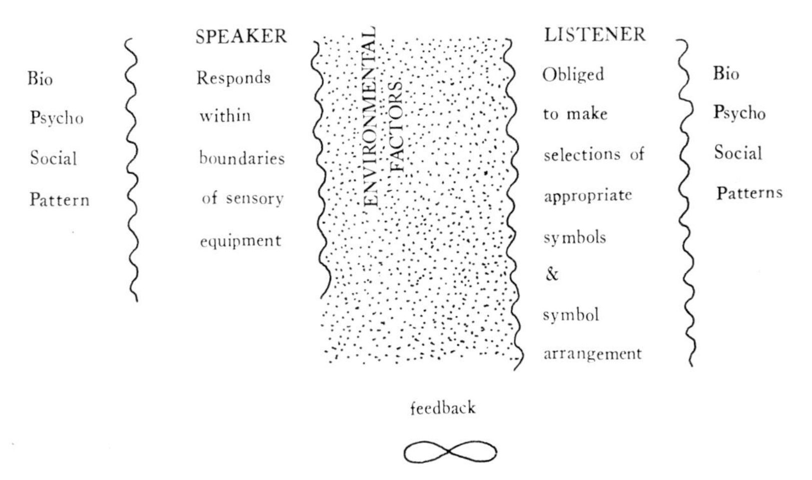

Figure 2. The communication cycle: influence of environment on interpersonal communication. (Modified from Russell Meyers, M.D., "Aphasia Shortcourse," unpublished papers, Institute of Logopedics, Wichita, Kansas, July 1950.)

is obliged to make a selection of appropriate symbols or ideas in order to respond. These responses are, again, altered by his biological and physiological states at the time of the utterance, by the social restrictions placed on the speaking situation, and by his ability to respond within the boundaries of his sensory equipment. This only serves to explain how the speaker relates to the listener and the listener to the speaker. It does not explain how the idea is developed prior to utterance. Although specifics of concept development will be discussed in detail later in the book, the following schemata will illustrate how attitudinal sets alter the exchange between speaker and listener.

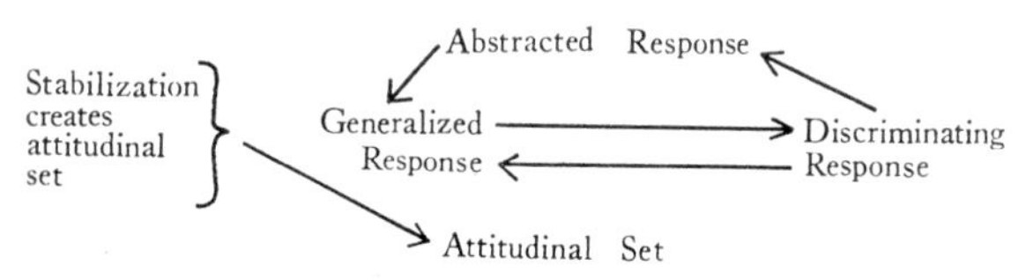

Figure 3. The development and interrelationship of attitudinal sets and conceptualization. (Modified from Russell Meyers, M.D., "Aphasia Short-course," unpublished papers, Institute of Logopedics, Wichita, Kansas, July 1950.)

First of all, the speaker has a general idea. This general idea needs to be interpreted to a particular listener. So, the speaker must select from a number of concepts, that specific concept that can be interpreted by the listener. He makes a discriminating response. This discriminating response has to be transferred into a level of abstraction that is most suitable for this speaking situation. His ability to select what is good, bad or indifferent for a particular speaking situation depends upon his attitudes about that situation. These attitudes are formed from previous experiences in similar situations. In other words, he has a preconceived image of how he functions in this particular speech situation. He has attitudes based (stabilized) on previous experiences and self-image.

As noted earlier, self-image influences reception and transmission of ideas and self-images are developed through social pressures. Any attempt to study the development of language must also include the study of environment. This study would include how the environment functions in influencing the child's need to develop self-help skills, motor skills, finer motor coordination, and some degree of creativity. All of these provide the necessary experiences that aid in the development of a more complex language system.

Verbal Skills

The final aspect of language that hampers our study of the subject *is our insistence upon viewing language as a completely verbal skill.* Communication need not be verbal. Music, art, gesture, anything that communicates an idea, is language. It is a transmissable signal. Certainly, the child does not rely solely upon verbal skills to interpret the world. A child may be able to tell you something is going wrong in the family without being able to verbalize what exactly is wrong. He interprets the atmosphere of the environment, less through words than he does by observing gestures, body attitudes and other visible signs of communication. For example, the amount of noise generated while mother sets the table is as much a clue as the words she uses during this task. Language is a term applied to a system of symbolic habits which each individual learns with such apparent ease that he cannot remember its beginnings. It involves all aspects of his expression from gesture, music, art and sculpture to conventional rules of grammar. The study of language should not concern itself solely with the capacity (vocabulary) of any particular individual but should be concerned with the functional utilization of communication on all levels of awareness, be it acoustical, graphic, or motorical.

In summary, then, remember that any study of language as a total phenomenon must consider the following:

1. Language is a search for self.
2. Research is prone to remove speech from the speaker and view it as a "pure" phenomenon.
3. Researchers are prone to associate language with their own experiences and therefore make value judgments.
4. Cultural impress governs our communication effectiveness.
5. Both the speaker and the listener have a role in communication.

6. Language need not be verbal.

This chapter attempts to note the complexity of language in order to make the reader aware of those factors that may influence his thoughts on language, whether or not those factors are the results of ideas propagated in grades K through twelve, or by "word of mouth" through family and friends. Although it appears that I have made it virtually impossible for you to view language with any degree of objectivity, that is not the case. On the contrary, it is particularly imperative that I enumerate those obstacles to objectivity in reference to this area of study.

Most young adults, until they have been parents or "mother"

The integration of language comprehension and experimental exploration begins with that first "step." (Courtesy Wood Photographs)

figures, tend to regard the infant as an amorphous creature who is subject to, but not a part of, this world. Most parents and child researchers are more than willing to argue to the contrary. Much of what the child sees and hears while in the crib is a mystery to the adult. Although children are somewhat alike, by size and stages of maturation, each assumes his own individual characteristics and each sees something quite different in his view from the crib. The child makes his first step toward individuality long before he gains his walking shoes.

His first smile of recognition when mother enters the room is one of the initial overt signs of individuality. (Obstetric nurses will tell you that even the new born has overt characteristics of individuality.) The child's awareness of the room itself helps shape his individuality. It is important then, to understand that the process of language begins long before the utterance of that first word. We will, in the next few chapters, discuss both the process as well as the results of the preverbal years. We will also trace the initial stages of language development as both a receptive and expressive developmental pattern. As the first step toward understanding child language, the next chapter will emphasize the four basic requirements for language.

Chapter Two

LANGUAGE ACQUISITION–LEARNED VERSUS INNATE

IN view of the discussion of the previous chapter, it is obvious that any attempt to trace the development and acquisition of speech in Man would constitute more than this volume, and a lifetime of controversy. Unfortunately, I cannot say that defining the development of child language will be any easier. The first step in that direction is to attempt to trace the child's acquisition of language. In that area, I prefer to accept what I call the "mama" theory of language acquisition. This theory, simply stated, is that the child initially produces sounds on a primary level in response to internal stimulation rather than external-environmental stimulation. He coos, mews, and cries. He refines movements of the oral mechanism that will be later used for speech.

Although these sounds cannot be characterized by the features of speech sounds (Deese, 1970), they are essential to speech sound production. Some time during this primary period (four to six months) sound becomes pleasurable and he reacts to the external awareness of his own productions. The child recognizes that *he* is making noise. This is much like the startled recognition of an adult who, during the asthmatic stages of a lingering cold, realizes that the wheezing he hears is his own. Finally, the child begins to react to the environment (external stimulation), which is in most cases, his mother. This occurs not by plan but by proximity. "Mother" is used here to mean the individual who keeps the infant clean and fed.

PREVERBAL STAGE OF DEVELOPMENT

Now "mother" becomes more than good food and a clean bottom, but warm hands, a familiar smell, and voice as well. The child has yet to see her as having feet, nor is he concerned about her dress or hairdo. He is aware of her voice as his ear lies next to her breast. "Mother" has become familiar bits and pieces, but it will be some time before she is recognized as a complete individual, feet and all.

The infant does not arrive in this world with a perception of his body or body image. ". . . at birth there is no indication that the infant knows either self or objects. His first adaptations to the environment are in the form of reflex movements such as sucking, grasping, and eye movements" (Furth, 1969). Body image is not at first a visual one; it is a verbal construct built out of names and commands (Brown and Van Riper, 1966). These verbal constructs are experienced by the child as a part of his daily routine; mother's talking as she diapers, bathes, feeds him. Let us imagine that the infant in the crib sees something waving around some distance from him. It seems to come around every day and when he gets tired, it goes away. One day, he eats it! He can *taste* it and *feel* himself tasting it. He discovers that *he* can make *it* move. "More striking still is the baby's discovery of his feet, which he treats as alien entities which sometimes drift into view and which his active hands capture and bring to his mouth for testing" (Church, 1961). Eventually, mother's mumblings about "foot" will be connected to this thing that he has "discovered," but now the great joy is that he can manipulate it at will.

During this period, he also learns to manipulate his articulators. His vocalizations become more repetitive. Vowel sounds, although still predominant, diminish in proportion to the number of consonant sounds. He begins to combine sounds and uses sound combinations more frequently. He appears to enjoy his manipulations and experiments with sounds. Eventually, these sounds become more syllabic in nature. The repetitions increase and certain combinations are used more frequently than others. During this period of repetition or babbling (six to nine months), the baby receives some reinforcement from the environment. Although there have been some contradictory reports as to the benefits of babbling behavior (Myklebust, 1961; Winitz, 1961),

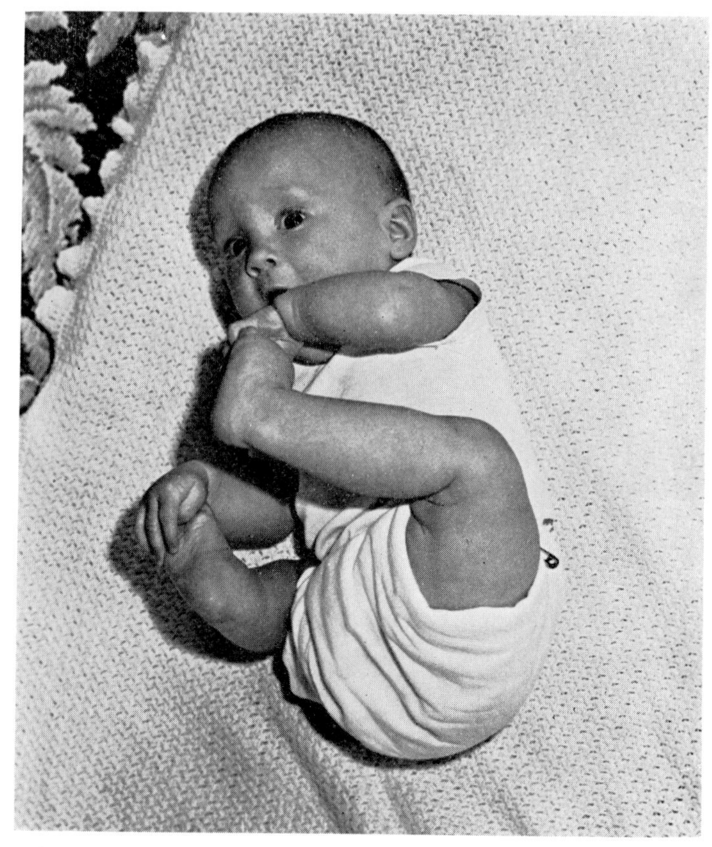

Those first discoveries require the "taste-test." (Courtesy Wood Photographs)

it would appear that the greatest benefit during this period is in the development of control over the articulators.

The very nature of his daily activities reinforces some sound productions. As a result, he may produce bilabial sounds while sucking and eating. The lingering pleasure of a good meal prolongs this activity. Other sounds are stimulated by tactile association. The state of his internal reactions are geared more toward the production of certain sounds than toward others. If the baby is in discomfort, he will cry more, and during that period produce more vowels. When he is satisfied and comfortable, more consonant activity may be noted. Lewis (1963) has conducted research regarding the significance of crying activity to speech sound production. Lewis stated that discomfort cries produced more narrow, tense sounds, thereby limiting speech sound production. Although not all researchers agree with Lewis' findings it would seem plausible that certain crying activity (particularly comfort cries) is more conducive to speech sound production than other cries (involving generalized activity and frustration).

Regardless of the lack of agreement among researchers about the value of the babbling activity, the final product of the babbling stage (at approximately twelve months), sounds something like "mama" or "dada" in almost any language. In the Ural Mountains of Russia, in Bantu country, in Watts, or in surburbia U.S.A., "mama"or "dada" are reported most often as the first recognizable words. Lewis (1951) found mama, dada, nana, tata, papa, to be international in the language of babies. Almost every language has a similar word denoting parent.

The child at this stage can be thought of as multilingual, for he indeed, in his repertoire of sounds, has the *potential* sound system of any and all languages. The ability to retain, use, and discard sound combinations depends on (a) the type of reinforcement offered by the environment, (b) his ability to learn from his experiences, and (c) his ability to develop the necessary skills to maintain this production potential during the maturational process. He learns, eventually, that language helps catalog the world. Language helps bring similarities and differences into focus. It is an efficient and expedient method of dealing with friends and family. Most of all, the child learns that language can be used for comparing perceptions and making order out of chaos.

Contradictions

This view is not shared by all researchers of language acquisition. Most agree that the period of onset is universal. "Apparently no field worker has ever been struck by any discrepancies between vocalizations or communicative behavior among children of 'primitive' and 'western' man" (Lenneberg, 1966). However, not all agree as to the cause of the onset or its subsequent development.

The trend of research can be capsulized in the following manner. There are researchers, such as McNeill (1970), who propose that language is innate; that man is destined to be verbal. There are others, such as Skinner (1957), who insist that language is a learned tool and that certain environmental controls precipitate this learning. The first group of researchers defend their views by stating that any child is capable of learning language under any set of circumstances. They cite instances of children who have managed to learn language under the most hostile set of circumstances (usually this includes economic level although no one has proven a one-to-one relationship between wealth and words—"When I get some more money, I'll talk better"). The second set of researchers cite cases of "wolf boy" and other children abandoned or confined in isolation who have not developed speech as a part of the "natural" order of events.

These views have not been resolved to date. The "innate" researchers continue to insist that language is a predestined tool of man, a built-in device. They concede that reinforcement must occur so that the child can be provided with some means of testing those possibilities supplied by his built-in "device" (Deese, 1970). The "learned" researchers continue to insist that it is governed by the environment's influence on the child's abilities. Furthermore, the latter group fails to agree on just how this development occurs.

In general, it has been hypothesized that development occurs as the result of one of four possible conditions. First of all, development has been hypothesized to be an "individual" task in that the child adapts his own plan to the requirements of the environment. Development is also considered to be "unified" by some and "dynamic" by others. The former implies that the plan is a sequence of phrases, harmonized (like so many voices in chorus); while the latter implies that each phase is altered by past experiences, personality, and ego development. A fourth hypothesis, that of "continuity" appears to be almost an outgrowth of the dynamic theory of development. The continuity hypothesis is that the child's development has continuity; i.e. early behavior trends and patterns persist (perhaps the most

Freudian-like of all the views). Now let us take a closer look at these hypothesized theories of language development.

HISTORICAL OVERVIEW

Bloomfield (1927), Skinner (1957), and Staats (1968) are among the theorists who believe that language is governed by a series of responses to stimuli. They hypothesize that there is no universal grammar and that language is learned as a species-specific behavior through operant conditioning in which the parent is the conditioning agent. Chomsky (1957) and McNeill (1970) are among those who state that language (although it is a species-specific function) is universal. There are hierachical and multileveled rules for developing grammar that are present in all languages. The child develops language because he is innately equipped to do so. The environment helps him further structure a task that is built into his biological/neurological mechanism.

On the other hand, Piaget (1959) and his followers state that language can be defined only in terms of the cognitive framework of the child. The conceptual and perceptual organization is influenced by the child's intellectual character. Language develops along with, and is influenced by, his capacity to adapt to the environment through logical thought, judgment, and reasoning.

Whorf (1956) and others view language as a reflection of culture. It helps shape and is shaped by the culture. Words and objects are associated and language is required as a social necessity. Before you can understand language you must understand the culture. The reverse is true as well. Both Piaget and Whorf felt that language was a species-specific function.

I would prefer to adopt the eclectic theory and assume that language acquisition is a combination of all of these arguments. Language is both innate and learned. It is also governed by developmental schedules that are inclusive of all of the views cited. The child must have the necessary tools for language acquisition, and he must have the wherewithal to use those tools. In addition, environmental stimulation and reinforcement must exist so that he can develop a language system that is *common* to his environment (both cultural and geographic). The child cannot proceed toward competence faster than his experiences will allow him. He cannot become competent with multisound combinations, such as consonantal blends, until he has achieved some degree of competence with those same sounds in less difficult consonant-vowel combinations. He cannot develop categorization and comparison concepts until he has achieved some competence in the use of identification and naming concepts.

BASIC REQUIREMENTS TO LANGUAGE

There are four basic requirements to language that should be discussed before we proceed to what constitues a language. These requirements are those skills needed for language that are in part maturationally controlled and in part environmentally controlled. Language is a species-specific characteristic. Some children, however, fail to develop this skill because of organic deficits (such as deaf or neurologically impaired children). Others fail because of environmentally imposed causes (such as institutionalized children). Still others fail for no obvious reason. It would seem that language is more likely to occur under certain conditions. The child must be able to hear, understand, and remember language events. He must also be able to initiate and experiment with these events as well as solve problems that occur as a result of language events. In other words, he must be able to audit language events, remember language events, have the opportunity to perform or use language, and have enough intelligence to utilize language as part of his problem solving methods.

Performance

Performance can be easily observed by just listening to the child. It does not mean counting words (capacity or vocabulary) but observing the child's ability to manipulate those words at his disposal in order to convey ideas appropriately to his audience. No two children behave in exactly the same fashion although their performances may be strikingly similar. Environmental factors such as familial, regional, and socio-economic conditions are involved. The most important aspect of performance is the child's ability to relate to those environmental factors; that is, the degree of egocentric and independent involvement.

The child spends much of his life developing self-concept. Self-concept is partially the outgrowth of body image. He uses language to further aid the development of self-concept. Body image and language help the child develop an awareness of himself in relation to the rest of the world. The very young child is egocentric in that he does not separate self from others. It is not that he is selfish but that he has a lack of self. He does not perceive objects or people as a whole but as parts; a string of singular events any one of which can indicate the whole. If he runs into a tree, he kicks the tree since it is nearest to the source of his pain. Until he develops a perception of the whole and can see things relative to their parts, the world is chaotic. He uses language as a part of the activity that will develop order out of this chaos. He develops what Strauss and Kephart (1955) call "roadsigns of words to keep himself oriented. Language for the young child is much more a process of pinning down his perceptions and stabilizing the world around him than communication with other individuals." He uses language egocentrically before he uses it in independent communication as would the adult. Until the child has developed this independent function, his language may tend to appear repetitious and limited in scope. His experimentations and questions (performance attempts), will enable him to expand the limitations of his language.

Audition

Another factor involved in learning language is feedback or auditorization. The child must be able to audit *his* production of sounds before he begins the process of shaping his repertoire of sounds into the environment's code of behavior. Speech sounds that are acquired first are those that are more tactile, visible, and require less coordination and expenditure of energy. They are also those that use movements more closely associated with eating movements. New sounds are developed syntagmatically (by adding two sounds together) or paradigmatically (substituting one sound or movement for another). Eventually the child learns which sounds are appropriate and which are not. If he is unable to audit what he hears, he may continue to produce the same combinations of sounds despite all efforts to correct him.

This is not just a difficulty in receiving sounds. The deaf child has a difficulty of receiving sounds. Many children without hearing losses have difficulty perceiving sound or auditing. Sensation or reception of sound is the ability to hear while perception is the process by which incoming stimuli are organized into patterns. Sensation is defined as an individual's first unlearned response to stimulation of his sense organs (Johnson and Myklebust, 1967). As one sensation is associated with another, the action between the central nervous system and the incoming impulse leads to an interpretation or perception of that stimulation. Deese (1970) stated that the child invents distinctions among the speech sounds he hears. In other words, he perceives a difference between these speech sounds and uses that difference to identify the sound. It is an invention only in that the child usually develops this sense of distinction on an individual basis without superimposed rules from the environment.

As each new sensory stimulus affects the child, he comes to perceive that each new experience is different from the former ones. This perception depends on what he hears when he says a sound as well as how it feels when he says it. Feeling or tactile audition is a proprioceptive function. It provides information about the position of the articulators during sound production. He alters his productions syntagamatically or paradigmatically in accordance with these perceptions. These alterations are audited through auditory and proprioceptive information. His performance improves as his audition improves. Through categorization the child can scan and compare his perceptions. Hearing and proprioception serve as a check-and-balance in the development of sound proficiency. He cannot use auditorization, however, without memory.

Memory

A third factor involved in learning language is memory. A child must perceive differences, audit the perception and remember the auditorization. He must be able to remember it long enough to produce it consistently. "We must imagine that the limitations of memory are important determiners of actual linguistic performance" (Deese, 1969). Memory span is defined as the ability to retrieve as well as to store. "Noise" plays an important role in this process. Noise is both external and internal interference and may be visual, tactile, or auditory. It can occur as background and/or foreground interference. Because of noise interference, storing and retrieving memory units involves attention. The young child has difficulty attending to stimuli because he is unable to separate foreground from background "noise." He is also involved in erratic movements which he has not yet learned to control and he has a low tolerance for stress.

As the child grows older, he is less subject to erratic movement and does not fatigue as rapidly. However, he still has a tendency to become fixated on details that may have no real bearing on the subject at hand. He also has not learned to work under group rules. Piaget (1954) states that the child, until he is approximately five years old or so, rarely interacts socially for any significant period of time. The young child most often adheres rather rigidly to an established routine (and outside of the immediate family, it is difficult to find such a routine). Another factor that hampers social interaction is the child's inability to suppress inappropriate responses. Any one of these factors could interfere with attention which in turn interferes with memory.

The child finds it difficult to attend because he is seldom inactive enough to attend. Input-output stimulation becomes the foreground "noise" against a background of activity already in progress. The child's language responses are directed toward preserving an identity in a chaotic world. Language is suited to the purpose of pulling out the more general similarities and differences and dealing with them as a group. In order to develop an awareness of likes and dislikes, the child must be able to attend without the constant distraction of details of any one experience. The child is caught in a circle of a multitudinous garble of sounds that we call language and his own lack of behaviorial controls. He must have a number of experiences with sounds and words before he can remember the appropriate response.

There is, as well, no way of predicting which details of an event the child will select for storage and how well he will be able to retrieve that unit. It is not only the nature of the child, but human nature that no two events will be viewed in the same way since the occurrence of one has altered all succeeding occurrences. This author remembers overhearing two children talk about eating ice cream. At the beginning of the conversation (and the beginning of the dish of ice cream), they both agreed that the best bite was the first one. At the end of the conversation (and the end of the ice cream), they both agreed that it depended on how well you liked what you were eating: "If it is good, the best bite is the first. But if it is not so good, the best bite is the last and you know there is no more in the kitchen."

Memory for language must be both short term and long term. Short term in that the child needs to remember the word or sound combination while still in the original situation. Long term memory refers to the ability to apply this word or sound combination to similar but not exact events in the future. In other words, he must store the memory so that he may retrieve it for identical events, but in order to develop a complex language system, he must be able to apply it appropriately to similar events.

Intelligence

The application of memory to events that are similar but not identical involves intelligence. Repetition or memory is an automatic response that does not involve cause-effect relationships. Repetition is operant in that the chain of events has been prescribed and learned in a prescribed manner. The child hears a word and repeats the word. He then is rewarded by mother's smile and his pleasure. This Pavlovian type response is most often used as an example of operant conditioning. Memory of appropriate responses for less than identical situations involves intelligence in that the individual must be able to perform an act involving the application of previously completed responses to a *new* set of circumstances. Intelligence, in this case, indicates that a child must have the capacity to generalize and restructure his language to fit many speech situations. This generalization and restructuring is both learned and developmental. Learned implies growth and that, in turn, involves experiences. Experiences lead to new structures and new structures are altered by memory. A child learns through experience to alter his responses.

Development implies that the sequence of altered events is governed by physical, cultural, and personality limitations. This sequence is relatively fixed. A child learns gross motor actions before he develops finer motor movements. Generalized concepts are learned before he develops qualifying ideas for that generalized concept. A child understands one-to-one relationships before he develops plurality. He understands the concept of yesterday and today before he fully understands verb tense. Everything that is man progresses from the gross to the finer, and everything that *is*, is significant if only we are equipped to interpret it.

Intelligence tests propose to measure capacity and/or competence when, in effect, they measure performance under a *fixed* set of circumstances. Tests fail to assess whether children are actually *not* capable of taking advantage of existing stimulation (Lenneberg, 1966) but instead measure their performance on a given day. Intelligence here, then, is defined as the child's ability to learn—the continuity of structuring that allows existing structures to be reformed by new experiences. Indeed, much of the educational process you are undergoing is an identification shift or restructuring that is the result of learning the language of the college environment in general and each course in particular.

In summary, the child has an innate ability for language and this ability is utilized through chance-by-chance discovery. Much of what we do to stimulate the development of language is not immediately used by the child. Some of these stimulations are incorporated into other areas of development, such as motor and social development. Our attitudes and ideas concerning food, clothing, and pleasure are internalized by the child to some degree while he is in the preverbal stage of development.

His experimentations during that period are as important to motor control as they eventually are to expressive language. The infant's vocalizations during the babbling period provide him with the experience necessary for eventual control over the articulators. It is also during this period that he discovers the pleasure of vocalization. His entire system is involved in those vocalization attempts. Any child "watcher" can comment on the

Figure 4. Much of what we come to know as "reality" begins with explorations in the crib (after Camper).

amount of motor activity, such as kicking the sides of the crib with arms waving, that accompanies babbling behavior. Language, like any other developmental process, is altered by the amount of stimulation provided by the environment.

As the child's vocalizations and receptive abilities become more refined, he learns to alter his verbal behavior in much the same manner as he learns to feed and dress himself. And, by the same token, he cannot learn to verbalize or feed and dress himself any faster than his level of maturation will allow. In all of these areas, children learn (a) that there are those things that are unimportant and can be ignored, (b) to change behavior when consistently reinforced (these changes are habitual, recognizable, and easily predictable), and (c) to experiment and compare percepts for those changes that are unforeseen and must be observed firsthand. It is through these last changes that the child learns to catalog future experiences.

Experimentation and adaptability to change keeps his language moving and growing. The next chapter will deal with the growth of expressive language behavior. Speech and language will be differentiated. The contents in that chapter should be viewed as a definitive basis for the process of cognitive, neurophysiological and psychosocial develpoment that will be discussed in future chapters.

Chapter Three

SPEECH PRODUCTION AND LANGUAGE UNITS

ONE researcher stated that "the developmental sequence followed rather definite stages, exhibited cross-cultural generality and involved a strong biological and neurophysiological basis" (Jakobson, 1968). However, before we proceed to a discussion of the sequence of language development from the standpoint of neurophysiological and social factors, it is necessary to discuss the elements of speech and language (the components of speech production and language expression). It is the purpose of this chapter, therefore, to briefly describe the properties of speech production and language units.

VOCALIZATION MECHANISM

It has been stated that the mechanism of the larynx was originally evolved as a valve to guard the entrance to the lungs and to regulate inspiration and expiration (inhalation and exhalation). In the course of further evolution, the larynx (by effecting a firm closure of the glottis, insured a fixed thorax. This provided a firm attachment for muscles of the arms and shoulder girdle, which was a great advantage for the primates.

Speech is a secondary function. The articulators (tongue, palate, and lips) are primarily suited for eating. The breathing apparatus regulates and sustains the oxygen intake. The resonators (notably the chest cavity, bones of the skull and muscles of the trunk) serve as connectors and as a part of motor functions. The wedge-shaped vocal folds serve as a safety valve to protect the lungs from infiltration by water and other foreign substances as well as an aid to help contain air within the lungs. In their secondary functions, the whole complex laryngeal frame of bones exists to enclose protectively, and to maintain efficient operation, of the vocal folds.

By referring to Table I, it is possible to get a cursory view of the functions of the speech production mechanism. The vocalizing mechanism, then, includes a respiratory process that provides an energy source; vocal folds that provide valvular vibration, resonating cavities above the vocal folds that provide sound modifying chambers; and articulators which alter the sounds reaching them by molding, separating or combining these sounds through interruptions or breath blockages.

Phonation

The vocal basis of speech is more than just laryngeal tone. Laryngeal tone is musical (periodic series of noises) or nonmusical (nonperiodic series of noises). This tone must be pro-

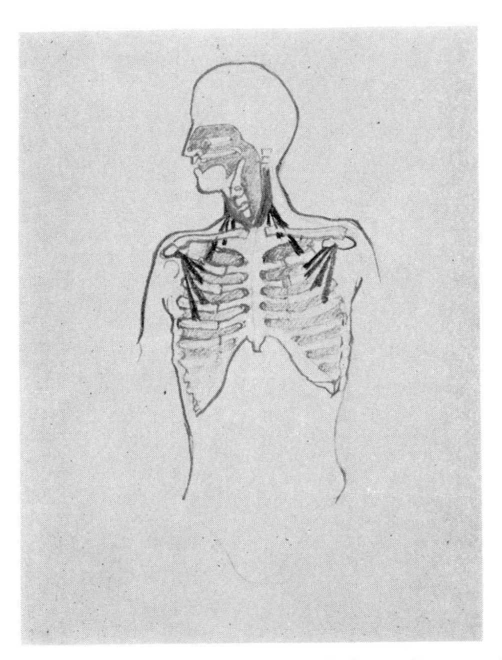

Figure 5. The upper respiratory system including the muscles of respiration and rib cage. (From Alfred Benninghoff, *Lehrbuch der anatomie des menschen,* II. © 1949. By permission of Urban and Schwarzenberg, München, Berlin.)

TABLE I
DIVISIONS OF SPEECH PRODUCTION SYSTEM AND THEIR RESPECTIVE FUNCTIONS FOR SPEECH

	Structures	*Functions*
Respiratory mechanism	1. Thoracic cavity	1. Generates expiratory air pressures and flows required at the larynx for phonation.
	2. Lungs and tracheo-bronchial tree	2. Generates oral air pressures required for consonant articulation.
	3. Neuromuscular systems which control the volume of the thoracic cavity.	3. Participates in control of pressure and flow required for regulation of vocal pitch and intensity and to divide speech into syllables and phrases, etc.
Laryngeal mechanism	1. Larynx (cartilages, folds, membranes, ligaments, etc.) both intrinsic and extrinsic.	1. Vocal fold vibrations provide quasi-periodic sound source during voice production.
	2. Neuromuscular systems for controlling adduction-abduction, lengthening-shortening, stiffening (tensing) and relaxing of vocal folds and for controlling gross movements of the larynx as a whole.	2. Laryngeal adjustments coordinate with intratracheal air pressure regulation to control vocal pitch and vocal intensity.
		3. Vocal fold action determines input acoustic spectrum to vocal cavities thus setting basic voice quality characteristics.
		4. Valving action assists in regulation of air flow during both consonants and vowels.

Vocal cavity system	1. Pharyngeal, oral and nasal cavities a. Pharyngeal walls b. Epiglottis c. Tongue, jaw, lips, hard and soft palate, pharyngeal walls, etc.	1. Articulation of vowels by a. Shaping of oral-pharyngeal tract to regulate resonance properties of tract. b. Controlling coupling to nasal cavities. 2. Articulating consonants by a. Generation of continuous spectrum noise by constricting air flow at various locations in oral tract. b. Generation of transient noises by stopping and sudden releases of air. c. Regulate coupling in nasal cavities. d. Control shaping of oral-pharyngeal tract to regulate resonance properties. 3. Assists in regulations of air flow through valving actions. 4. Participates in regulation of voice quality and vocal intensity.

From *Human Communication and its Disorders—An Overview*, National Advisory of Neurological Diseases and Strokes © 1969 by permission of National Institute of Public Health, Subcommittee on Human Communication and its Disorders, Bethesda, Maryland.

duced under certain conditions in order to insure efficient vocal quality. First of all, the tone must be produced under the conditions of an ideal glottis (opening between the vocal folds). These conditions are as follows:

1. The folds must have two edges that can be brought into exactly parallel approximation.
2. This approximation must be so close as to prevent the escape of any air except when driven by "real" chest pressure.
3. The approximation must not be so close as to prevent the free movement of the bands when set in vibration by the air stream.

Phonation is composed of a fundamental tone with overtones. The fundamental tone is one frequency of vibration which determines the pitch of your voice. Overtones or partials are not separate pitches but help to determine the distinctive quality of the voice you hear. The frequency of the vibration is measured in cycles per second, while the distance between frequencies is called the wavelength. High voices have shorter wavelengths than lower ones.

While frequency is determined by length, thickness, tension and density of the vocal folds, wavelength is determined by the extent of displacement of the vocal folds from their normal condition. When the edges of the folds are brought together, air pressure is built up beneath the glottis by the action of the muscles controlling exhalation. Because the vocal folds are taut, they resist this pressure and are forced apart by it, thereby setting them into vibration. Although vocal fold vibration determines pitch, voice quality characteristics are a combination of pitch and resonance.

Resonance

Resonance for speech can be described as the adjustment of the cavities of the body (especially in the region of the head and neck) so that air masses vibrating within these cavities during phonation will be sympathetic to certain partials of the sounds produced by the vocal folds. There are three major resonating cavities: oral, pharyngeal, and nasal. Other cavities of the body, particularly the trunk, assist in resonation. As the cavities change

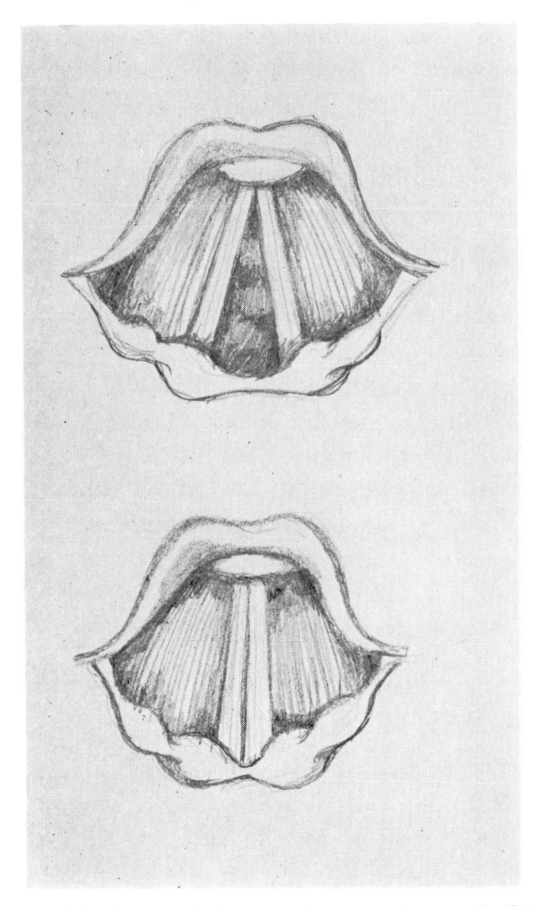

Figure 6. Vocal folds during (a) normal respiration, and (b) vocalization. (Adapted from Plate V, Volume 16, #3 CIBA Clinical Symposia, illustrated by Frank H. Netter, M.D.)

size and shape during speech production, they tend to resonate different partials (tonal qualities) of the phonated sound. The change in the relative size and shape of the resonating cavities not only determine which speech sounds are produced and amplified, but also enables us to recognize the paralinguistic elements of speech. Intonation, inflection, loudness, and emotional status of the speaker are the major paralinguistic elements.

Intonation patterns are used to indicate the intellectual and emotional content of the message. These patterns involved step changes or tonal movements from one message unit to another as well as movements within a message unit (sentence or phrase). The emotional status of the speaker my effect intensity of phonation (loudness), intonation, or pitch. The level of pitch at which we usually vocalize is referred to as habitual pitch. Although there may be a level at which phonation can be produced with a minimum of muscular action in an efficient and effective manner (optimum pitch), many speakers develop habit patterns phonation which are not considered optimal for their particular physical structure. When a speaker is excited, depressed or tense, he usually exhibits significant changes in pitch level. During this period, variations in pitch level are significantly different from optimum and/or habitual patterns. Under normal conditions, the speaker varies pitch level for intonation by adjusting the tone within a minimal range of frequences (step changes) but returns to his optimum and/or habital level after this excursion up or down the scale.

The frequency a cavity will resonate is determined by the mass of air within the cavity as well as the shape of the cavity. Resonance which *increases* the strength of certain frequencies is called "constructive interference" while resonance which produces a dampening or decreasing effect on frequency strength is called "destructive interference." In the latter instance, the resonating cavities tend to *reduce* the strength of certain frequencies, cancelling out partials of the phonated tone. By either method or by a combination of methods, we produce speech sounds composed of several relatively strong energy regions at specific frequencies. Much of what we recognize as individualized voice quality are the effects of resonance.

Respiration

Respiration is a vital part of vocal activity. The differences between normal quiet respiration and respiration for speech are as follows:

Normal:

1. Expiration equals that of inspiration.
2. Respiration is automatic and involuntary.

3. A relatively small amount of air is used.
4. Breathing takes place through the nose.

Speech:

1. Expiration time exceeds that of inspiration.
2. Respiration is partly under the control of consciousness.
3. A large amount of air is needed.
4. Breathing takes place through the nose and mouth, while the air stream is directed through the mouth.

Respiration consists of a two-phase cycle of inhalation and exhalation. Phonation rarely takes place during inhalation. Breathing for speech should simply include a sufficient supply of air that is unhindered in natural flow and can be easily controlled. Exhalation should be delivered in a smooth, sustained manner and without accompanying undue tensions. Except for nasalized sounds, the breath stream should be directed through the oral cavity.

To inhale, the air pressure within the lungs must be decreased in comparison with that outside the body. Exhaling is the opposite. The lungs always occupy all of the possible space within the thoracic cage. In order to increase their size, muscular contractions enlarge the thoracic cage, thereby increasing the volume and decreasing the pressure within that cavity. With the pressure decreased, air is taken in through the nasal passage. The reverse occurs during exhalation.

Respiration provides the motive power for speech. It activates the vocal folds and provides a stream of air that can be sent through narrow spaces, over sharp edges, or can be rapidly interrupted for the production of sounds containing elements of friction.

Articulation

The final aspect of speech activity is articulation. This is the process of stopping and/or interfering with the exhaled breath stream. This procedure may or may not be accompanied by phonation. Typical articulatory actions involve stoppage and release of air flow, forcing the air stream through narrow spaces, movement of the velum (soft palate) or closure of the nasopharyngeal port, and shaping of the resonating cavities.

While it is sometimes said that vowel sounds are resonated and that consonant sounds are articulated, the distinction is neither concise nor completely accurate. Since the articulators are active in adjusting the cavities for proper resonance of vowels, a vowel sound may be in a sense, "articulated." Perhaps it could be said that vowels are characterized by an uninterrupted flow of air with the articulators in a relatively static position, while consonants are characterized by a disturbed flow of air with the articulators in movement. Some speech sounds have the elements of both vowels and consonants and are called semi-vowels.

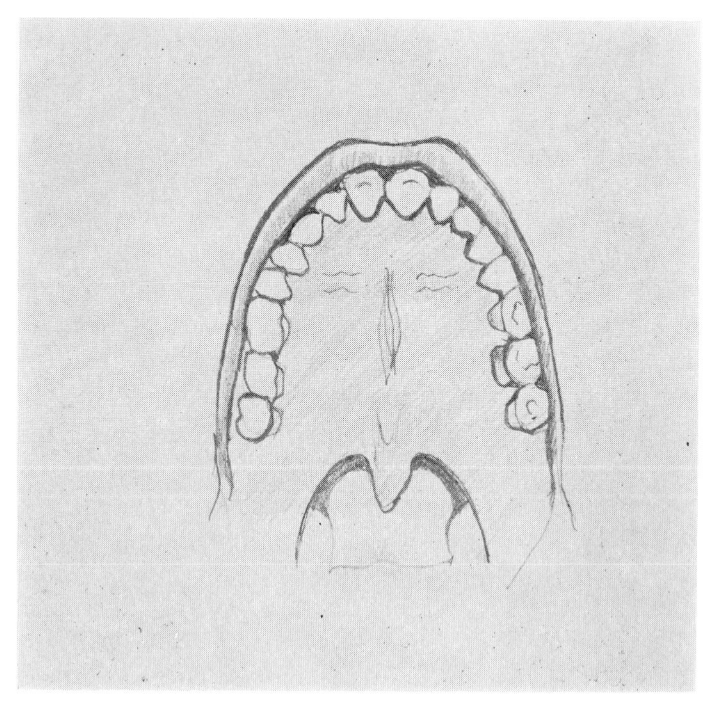

Figure 7. Structure of upper dental arch with view of hard palate and soft palate. (From Willard R. Zemlin, *Speech and Hearing Science: Anatomy and Physiology*, © 1968. By permission of Prentice-Hall, Englewood Cliffs, New Jersey.)

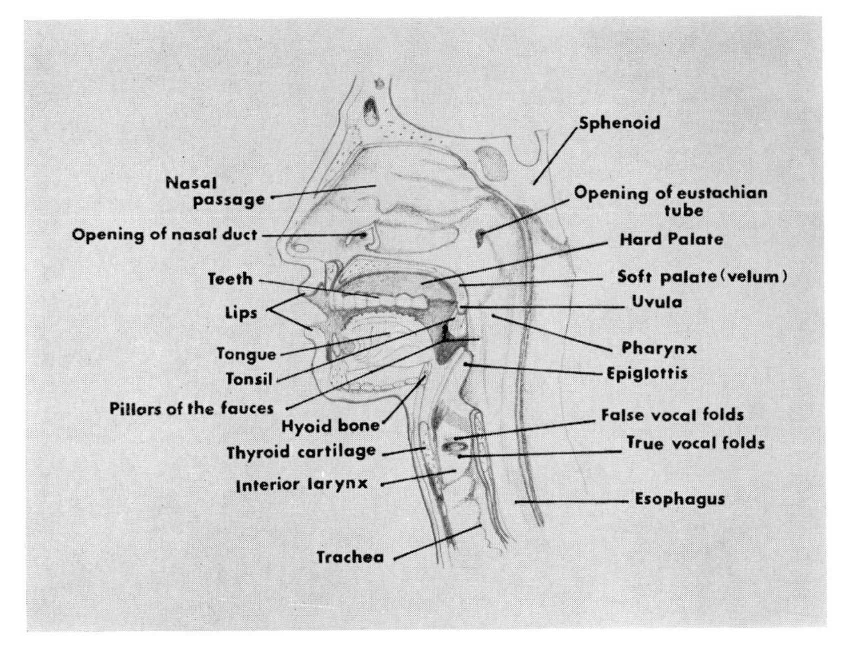

Figure 8. Saggital view of the head (after Camper).

Speech sounds are traditionally identified by formant and position. Formants are narrow bands of frequencies that sound something like musical tones. Formant characteristics are measured by spectographic techniques. The sound is recorded on this electro-acoustical device in graph form known as an acoustic spectrum. This allows us to note visually which frequencies are present and which are not during the production of certain sounds. The spectographic technique is used to analyze the formants that characterize word production as well as sound production.

Without sound spectograph information, speech sounds are classified by the relative position of the articulators. Vowels are described by tongue position, tongue tension, and lip position. Tongue height is the first aspect of vowel classification. The vowel is then described as "front," "back," or "central." The front vowels are those that involve the greatest activity in the blade of the tongue; central vowels, with activity in the medial or dorsal area of the tongue; and back vowels with activity in the

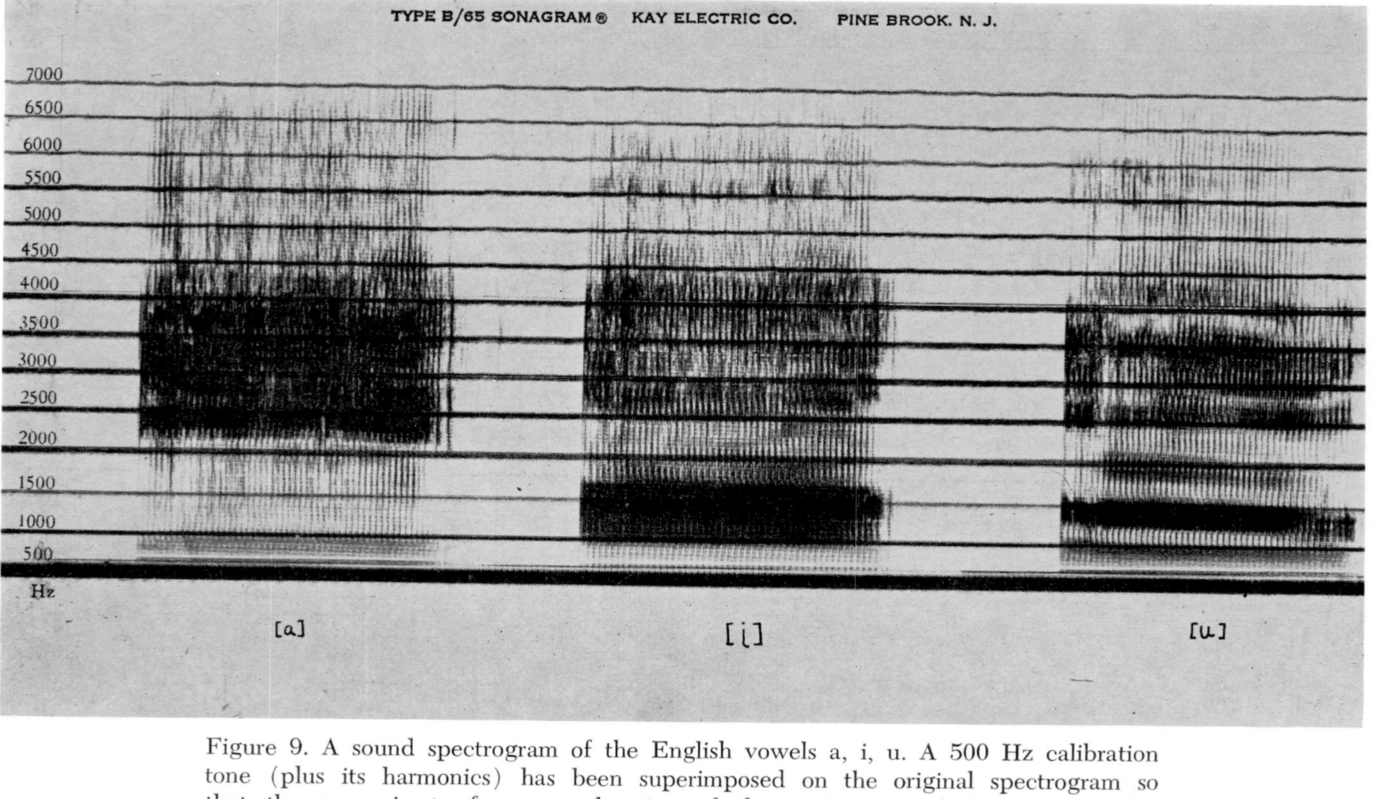

Figure 9. A sound spectrogram of the English vowels a, i, u. A 500 Hz calibration tone (plus its harmonics) has been superimposed on the original spectrogram so that the approximate frequency location of the various vowel formants can be more easily estimated. (Courtesy Western Washington State College, Speech and Hearing Clinic)

posterior section of the tongue. If the tongue is carried high during the production of a vowel, more tension is involved. Lip position refers to the relative size of the opening of the oral cavity. A rounded vowel, therefore, refers to the necessary lip position needed to produce that vowel. Back vowels involve more rounding than other vowels, while central vowels are more lax and relatively unrounded compared with other vowels. All vowels are voiced. The following chart is a summary of vowel placement for English vowels.

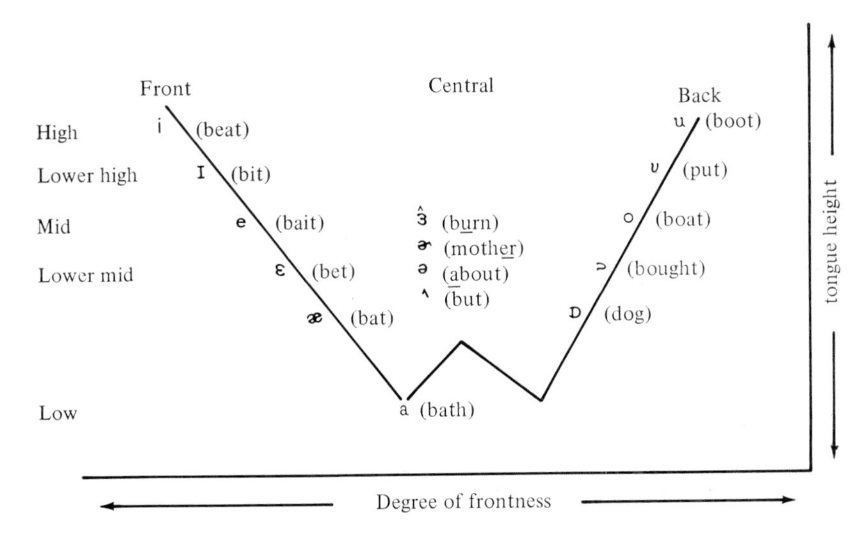

Consonants are also described by position. There are six general classifications of consonants delineated by the manner in which the exhaled air is altered. Plosive sounds are those sounds in which the air stream is completely blocked and then released suddenly. Fricatives are those sounds in which friction noises occur as a result of constricting the escaping air stream. An affricative is a sound that utilizes the movements of the plosive and the fricative. Nasals are the only sounds that are emitted through the nose rather than through the mouth. Glides occur when there is movement of the tongue, lips, or both, as the sound is produced. Semi-vowels are those sounds that have syllabic character; that is, they need not have an accompanying vowel when they appear as a second, unstressed syllable.

Consonants are also classified by the presence or absence of vocal tone. Voiced or unvoiced production does not change the general classification but merely indicates phonation. The final method of consonant classification (aside from formant characteristics) is place of articulation. Consonants are described by the articulatory structures involved in their production as well as by general classification and phonation. Consonant production involves movement of the lips, lips and tongue, tongue and teeth, tongue against alveolar ridge, tongue against palate, tongue and velum, and movement of the glottis. Consonant sounds of English may be described in the following manner:

Plosives:

1. Bilabials involving contact between the two lips completely blocking the oral passage before a sudden release of air. The position for the *b* voiced and *p* unvoiced as in *b*it and *p*an.
2. Lingua-alveolars involving contact between the tongue and alveolar ridge completely blocking the oral passage before a sudden release of air. The position for *d* voiced and *t* unvoiced as in *d*ip and *t*op.
3. Lingua-velars involving contact between the back of the tongue and the soft palate completely blocking oral passage before a sudden release of air. The position for g voiced and *k* unvoiced as in good and *k*ing.

Fricatives:

1. Labiodentals involving directing air stream between loose contact lower lip and of upper teeth. The position for *v* voiced and *f* invoiced as in *v*ine and *f*it.
2. Lingua-alveolars involving directing a narrow air blade against the cutting teeth. The tongue is grooved with the sides held against the molars tightly. The position for the voiced *z* and the unvoiced *s* as in *z*ip and *s*ee.
3. Lingua-palatals involving directing wide air blade between teeth as the sides of the tongue are held in loose contact with molars and middle area is raised toward palate. The position for *sh* unvoiced and *zh* voiced as in *shoe* and *azure.*
4. Lingua-dentals involving contact between the sides of the

tongue and edges of upper and lower teeth except for a small area of loose contact between edge of upper front teeth and tongue tip. Position for voiced and unvoiced *th* as in *th*en and *th*in.

Affricatives:

Lingua-palatals involving initial contact between tip of tongue and anterior hard palate. Tongue tip is then dropped immediately preceding expulsion of air between the teeth. The position for unvoiced *ch* and voiced *dz* as in *ch*ip and *j*am.

Nasals:

1. Bilabial contact between the two lips completely blocking the oral passage as the sound is emitted through the nose. Position for *m* as in *m*an.
2. Lingua-alveolar contact between the back of the tongue and alveolar ridge completely blocking the oral passage as the sound is emitted through the nose. Position for *ng* as in si*ng*.
3. Lingua-velar contact between the tip of the tongue and the hard palate completely blocking the oral passage as the sound is emitted through the nose. Position for *n* as in *n*o.

Glides:

1. Bilabial movement involving widening the labial orifice during the act of phonation that must start from a relatively small and rounded aperture. The position for *w* as in *w*ide.
2. Lingua-palatal movement involving widening of the aperture between the dorsum of the tongue and the hard palate during act of phonation that must start from a relatively narrow lingua-palatal aperture. Position for *j* as in *y*ellow.

Glottals:

1. Voiceless glottal fricative in which there is relatively little oral activity and the exhaled stream of air is emitted forcibly without vocalization. Position for *h* as in *h*ill.
2. Bilabial combination of the glide *w* and the glottal *h*. *h* is produced while the lips are in a relatively small and rounded position immediately followed by a widening of the labial orifice to produce *w*. Position of *wh* as in *wh*en.

Semi-vowels:

1. Lingua-alveolars involving medial contact between the tongue tip and the alveolar ridge so as to force a lateral emission of air during phonation. The *l* as in *l*ip involves a gliding action while second, unstressed syllabic *l* as in app*le* is characterized as a semi-vowel. When the tongue tip is in contact with the hard palate such as in ca*ll*, it is referred to as a "dark" *l* since spectographic recordings for this latter *l* appear to be much darker than other *l* sounds.

2. Lingua-palatals involving contact between the sides of the tongue and the maxillary dental arch, with the tongue tip or some portion of the dorsum of the tongue projecting up into the vault of the palate; only a narrow central opening. The tip of the tongue should be raised toward the anterior portion of the hard palate and curled slightly back. Position for *r* as in *r*ed.

Other types of sounds predominately used in English are blends (double or triple consonant combinations) and dipthongs (a glide from one vowel to another, during the production of which the position of the tongue changes).

ARTICULATION PROFICIENCY

The child's proficiency in the area of speech sound production is measured by the number of sounds that he articulates *correctly* based on adult proficiency standards. The term correctly indicates that the child must produce all the sounds that occur in a particular word or words as would an adult for those same words. From the previous description, it is easy to see that some sounds would be less difficult to produce than others. Fritz Schultz (Bar-Adon and Leopold, 1970), stated in 1880 that children initially acquire those sounds which would constitute a minimum expenditure of energy. Schultz's "law" was generally accepted as an explanation of sound production acquisition until research indicated that some children were able to produce the sounds in isolation or coincidently but not in specific word combinations. Other children appear to be virtually unable to produce some of these sounds although no anatomical explanation could be found for their lack of success.

Some research would lead us to believe that children find it difficult to monitor (audit) some sounds although they have no difficulty receiving (hearing) sounds. There are those children who have relatively little difficulty discriminating sounds but appear to be unable to articulate sounds because of the lack of proprioceptive information. Proprioceptive information implies knowledge about the relationship of certain parts of one's own body to other parts primarily through tactile sensations. The sounds that appear to be most difficult are those that lack definite articulatory contact and/or involve several coordinated movements of the articulators. These sounds are also less visible in that they involve movements that cannot easily be seen during production. Research indicates the *s, th, r,* and *l* are most frequently misarticulated, for example, among primary grade children (Karlin, Karlin and Gurren, 1965; West and Ansberry, 1968).

It would appear that Schultz was partially correct. Difficult sounds do require a maximum expenditure of energy but they also require auditorization and maximum use of proprioceptive information. These last two factors are skills that must be developed. These skills require attention and the complex use of perceptual information.

As the child is in the process of acquiring those skills that will lead to sound production proficiency, he tends to make four following kinds of "errors": (a) substitutions (another sound is substituted for the correct sounds), (b) omissions (the correct sound is omitted), (c) distortion (the correct sound is attempted but the attempt is not completely successful), and (d) addition (the correct sound is present but is articulated in combination with another sound not normally occurring in that position) (Van Riper, 1963).

Templin (1952) has conducted extensive studies in the area of articulation skills of young children. The Templin norms, as with any normative data, should not be considered as absolute cut off points but as guides to speech sound *proficiency.* It should also be noted that although Templin described her subjects in terms of socioeconomic level, she used standard English as proficiency level. The social implications of this research will be discussed in Chapter Seven. Some of Templin's findings indicate the following:

1. In the early years, dipthongs, vowels, consonant elements, double consonant blends, and triple consonant blends are produced in that order from most to least accurate.
2. The order of accuracy of articulation of consonant elements, from most to least accurate is as follows: nasals, plosive, fricatives, combinations, and semi-vowels.
3. The mean percentage of correct utterance is somewhat greater for the initial and medial than for the final position of the consonant elements.
4. There is a tendency for voiceless consonant elements to be produced somewhat more accurately than voiced ones, although this does not hold similarly for fricatives, plosives, and specific sound pairs. The unvoiced fricatives are produced significantly more accurately than the voiced fricatives at most age intervals. The voiced plosives, however, tend to be produced more accurately but not at a statistically significant level.
5. From ages three through six years, there is little change in the proportion of error in the initial, medial or final positions. At ages seven and eight, proportionately more errors occur in the medial than in the final position. This may be partially a reflection of the number of errors at those older ages in the articulation of *wh* sounds, which are measured only in the initial and medial positions.
6. Omissions increase substantially from the initial to the medial to the final positions; defective sound errors exhibit the same trend but to a lesser degree; substitutions, however, decrease in occurrence from the initial to the medial to the final positions.
7. The percentage of errors of omission decreases with age, but there is little relation to age in errors of substitution or defective sounds.
8. Sound discrimination ability shows a consistent increase with age, but its rate of growth is decelerated at about four and one-half to five years of age.

It is imperative to mention here that any evaluation of speech sound production proficiency in children must be conducted within the context of that child's envionment. By this I mean that a child of the Eastern area, for example, may appear to have some speech sound production errors if judged by Western or

Southern standards. Dialect codes involve definite phonological shifts as well as semantic and often syntactic shifts. Dialect influences will be discussed in a later chapter.

It is also important to note that the lack of proficiency in the production of some sounds will distort overall intelligibility of speech more than other sounds. The frequency of occurrence of sounds in the utterance of language units may influence the amount of intelligible speech that a child can produce. The chart below indicates frequency of occurrence for consonant sounds in adult standard English. Note here that some of the sounds cited by Templin as most difficult are also the ones that occur most frequently.

p, b, m	9.2%
f, v	5.6%
th voiced, *th* unvoiced	4.2%
t, d, s, z, n, l, r	60.7%
sh, dz, ch, zh, j	2.4%
k, g, w, ng	13.7%
h	4.1%

From *Working With Aspects of Language* by Mansoor Alyeshmerni and Paul Taubr, by Harcourt Brace Jovanovich, Inc., 1970 and reprinted with their permission.

Implications of Proficiency Thesis

The following examples are illustrations of the influence of frequency of occurrence and speech sound development on overall intelligibility. First, let us compare two statements:

(a) "What is this thing?"—adult
"Wah is dis fing?"—child
omission of final *t*
d substitution of initial *th*
f substitution of initial *th*

(b) "Let me play with the telephone."—adult
"Yet me pay wi di tehfone."—child
j substitution for initial *l*

p substitution for initial *pl*
omission of final *th*
d substitution of initial *th*
omission of medial *l*

Both utterances A and B made by a child contain many misarticulations when compared to the adult utterances. Although statement A contains fewer substitutions, there are still some inconsistencies and omissions, as in statement B. If the Templin information were used to compare the proficiency of these two utterances, little difference would be noted.

(c) "Are you a teacher or a nurse?"—adult
"A you a techuh o a nuhs?"—child
omission of final *r*
omission of medial *r*

At first glance, the child's utterance in statement C would seem to indicate an equal lack of proficiency with either statements A or B. However, the child in statement C has difficulty with only one sound *r*, and that difficulty is consistent. According to the Templin norms, the *r*, a semi-vowel, would be the most difficult sound in the sequence of sounds acquired by the child. Therefore the child of statement C has less difficulty with sound proficiency but perhaps more difficulty with overall intelligibility since *r* is in that group of sounds occurring 60.7 percent of the time.

(d) "Yes, I can read good."—adult
"Yes, I can weed dood."—child
w substituted for initial *r*
d substituted for initial *g*

(e) "I was not ready to go to school on Tuesday"—adult
"I no go to kul on Tuday"—child
no instead of *was not ready*
k substituted for initial *sk*
omission of medial *s*
omission of medial *s*

It is necessary here to differentiate syntactic differences from articulation differences. The child producing the utterance for statement D has articulation proficiency difficulties, so does the child in statement E. The difference between the two children does not lie in the area of articulation proficiency but in the area of syntax differences. Child E does not approximate adult standard English patterns as well as demonstrating speech sound production differences. Yet the child in statement E has essentially the same amount (although with identical sounds) of articulation proficiency difficulties. Rarely, however, are the two children viewed as at the same stage of speech sound production. The listener (teacher, clinician, or parent) is often more prone to rate the syntax differences as part of the articulation difficulties of child E. Since the development of syntax is influenced by rules of linguistic development rather than by rules of articulation proficiency, this type of evaluation is erroneous.

ELEMENTS OF LANGUAGE

Assuming that the individual has the necessary tools to produce vocal tone and speech sound patterns, language elements should be considered. Remember that language is described as the transmission of utterances in an intelligible and meaningful fashion. These utterances are studied in units referred to as linguistic units. The properties of linguistic units are phonology, semantics morphology, and syntactics.

Phonology

Phonology is that area of language designated as containing the acoustical characteristics of speech. It is divided into segmental and suprasegmental phonemes. It is partially the sound system as previously described in this chapter under the section on articulation. Deese (1970) says that speech is segmented into discrete and separate sounds and that the phoneme or sequence of phonemes is one way of describing speech. Phonemes, then, are elements common to a group of sounds. Segmental phonemes are the vowels, semi-vowels and consonants. The other portion of phonology involves the suprasegmental phonemes or the stress, pitch and juncture features of an utterance.

A child imbeds the rules of competence long before performance reaches maximum. (Courtesy Wood Photographs)

Suprasegmental phonemes are used to define language in terms of pronunciation and intonation. Vetter (1969) describes each of these phonemes as having four levels or degrees. Pitch is defined as the relative tonal height of an utterance. English has a minimum emphasis on pitch. The degree of rising or falling pitch tends to vary with changes in intensity, rate and juncture. Stress or accent is the loudness difference, the relative degree of intensity of an utterance. It is usually involved in changes along with pitch and rate, contributing a great deal to overall intelligibility. Juncture is the suprasegmental phoneme that indicates transition from one utterance to another. Junctures are the points of pause in connected speech. Pitch and juncture provide the intonation patterns of English. The four degrees of stress, pitch, and juncture are summarized as follows:

Primary stress:	/ ´ /
Secondary stress:	/ ` /
Tertiary stress:	/ ^ /
Weak stress: no mark or	/ ˘ /
Highest pitch level–extra emphasis:	/ 4 /
High pitch level–emphasis:	/ 3 /
Natural or habitual pitch level:	/ 2 /
Lowest pitch level–terminals:	/ 1 /
Juncture at a rising terminal:	/ ↗ /
Juncture at a falling terminal:	/ ↘ /
Juncture at a level terminal:	/ → /
Internal juncture:	/ + /

Variation in levels of emphasis and pitch and various kinds of pauses contribute to the meaning of an utterance. There are, of course, some properties involved in this area that are of particular concern to the phonetician or the descriptive linguist. For the student of language acquisition, however, the preceding section will suffice for an initial description of these features.

Semantics

Semantics involves meanings of words; categories, relationships, and contrasts. The child, like the adult, uses meaning to differentiate animate and inanimate objects. Slobin (1966) is quoted as saying, "It seems to me more reasonable to suppose that it is language that plays a role in drawing the child's attention to the possibility of dividing nouns on the basis of animation; or verbs on the basis of duration, or determinancy, or validity; or pronouns on the basis of social status, and the like." However, the child, unlike the adult, tends to use words on a much broader scale than does an adult. This is known as *holophrastic* utterance in which a single word utterance has a diffuse number of meanings (McNeill, 1970). "Baby?" may mean "There's another baby," or "Is that my toy?" The adult, on the other hand, has a number of words within each category that might be used interchangeably or to establish distinct differences within categories. The adult is more concerned with the qualities of utterances in that he has more words to handle those distinct differences of concepts (semantic distinction features).

The child is influenced by the adult in his choice of holophras-

Suprasegmental phonemes may be marked in the following manner:

Primary stress:	´ball
Secondary stress:	the ˊball
Primary and secondary stress:	the ´big ˋball
Primary, secondary and tertiary stress:	the ´big^gest ˋball
Primary and secondary stress:	´I will play ˋball (I don't care what you other guys do)
Primary stress:	I ´dropped the ball (usually I catch very well)
Weak or primary stress:	I'll play ´house (since no one else will play ball)
Falling terminal:	~~Katie has the ball~~ ↘
Rising terminal:	↗Oh! (I never knew that)
Falling terminal:	No ↘way! (not under any circumstances)
Level and falling terminal:	Mama went shopping → but didn-t take me↘
Internal juncture:	Mc+´Elroy ´Mcelroy
	Where (2) is (2) the (2) ball? (3) (how should I know?)
Emphasis:	He's (1) your (4) dog, (3) Charlie (2) Brown (2) (you know better than I)
	The (2) test (2) is (3) today (1) (now will you believe me?)

tic utterances. Braine (1970) reports teaching a two-year-old the words "seb" (as a noun) and "miss" (as a verb). The effect was that she used these words appropriately, developing a number of semantic relationships with the original concept category for the words. Her use of these utterances, however, was not entirely semantic but involved syntactic language properties as well. The development of semantic properties cannot be separated from cognitive development and categorization of information (see Chapter Five). Therefore, one of the characteristics of holophrastic utterances is that they are not only semantic units but syntactic units as well.

Not all theorists agree entirely with this description of childhood language. Goldstein (1948) used the terms "concrete" and "abstract" in his explanation of language disorders. He stated that concrete categories included naming activity, questions, and demands, whereas abstract categories include information that will be adapted to influence and inform the listener. Roger Brown (1958), DeVito (1970), and others, believe that children are more often involved in the activity of naming things. DeVito (1970) states that although children do learn their vocabulary from the abstract to the concrete, in most cases they are involved in concrete behavior since they are rarely, if ever, given abstract terms, such as quality, concept, or mineral, for a class of things. Their use of abstractions are in the form of generalizations rather than abstract terms. All that this attempts to do is emphasize that children place a wider variety of meaning on one term than do adults. Their abstractions are in the form of naming behavior. Moreover, children are usually given terms that provide immediate and essential information i.e. rock, truck, rather than terms such as mineral or transportation that are not specific enough to be descriptive without further explanation.

At first glance, it would appear that the concrete-abstract definition is far removed from the holophrastic utterance definition of childhood grammar behavior. Such is not the case. All the latter definition does is add to the list of terms used to describe language behavior in which one word serves several grammatical functions.

That the child appears to attend to naming categories prior to attempts at other categories is also supported by Ervin-Tripp (1970). Her research findings point out that children respond to "what" questions at an earlier age than for other types of questions. These responses developed soon after or concurrently with responses to yes-no questions. The child next developed the ability to respond to "where" and "what-do." All of these responses were acquired before the third year. After the third year the child gained the ability to respond to "who," "why," and "how." These responses required more complex ideas and the use of abstract generalizations. For example, (using a picture book) "Why is the deer going to eat?" is more complex than "Who is petting the deer?" All of the later responses demanded that the child anticipate events and/or generalize from past events. Although Ervin-Tripp believes that her sample is small and that some children will undoubtedly progress in some areas faster than in others, this research would seem to support the previous concrete-abstract discussion.

Skinner (1957) divided all speaking into two categories: tacts (statements) and mands (utterances for control). He stated that mand speech is more likely to be self-rewarding because of the reinforcement it receives: "Wait!" for example, is followed by a cessation of activity, and "OH-OHH!" by immediate searching. Much of the language behavior of the young child is of this sort. Mand utterances such as "candy?" receive some sort of immediate reinforcement. Every child learns to respond to and use "no-no." Skinner also uses the term echoic to describe repetitive responses. These responses normally become mands through reinforcment. The grammatic responses of the parent used to shape and expand language is termed autoclitic by Skinner. When the child responds to autoclitic language he is reinforced. Any behavior which gets such reinforcement is likely to appeal to the youngster enough so that he will sustain or elaborate on the behavior. This type of theory is the basis for the stimulus-response theories. However, S-R theorists cannot account for language behavior that appears despite, or in the absence of, specific autoclitic language. The lack of predictability of the amount of input actually used was evidenced by Smith (1970). This aspect of language acquisition will be discussed later in this chapter under the section "Competence vs. Performance."

Since the child's language behavior encompasses distinctions that are not adult-like (in that they are not clearly semantic or syntactic), the holophrastic utterance approach would seem feasible. Although we are fairly certain that the child is reinforced by the type of input, we cannot draw a direct correlation between autoclitic responses and language development.

Syntactics

Syntax is the principle that governs the ways in which words can be arranged together to form meaningful groups; rules for word combinations and order. Many researchers tend to completely ignore the fact that the basic properties of the child's language system differ greatly from the properties of the adult's language system. It would be fruitless, as McNeill (1966) pointed out, to try to "plug in" a different method of manipulation of concepts into a "standard." This is not only true for the description of the child's method of manipulation, but also for attempts to describe dialect differences. To attempt such a description in that manner would naturally reveal inadequacies, since the difference can never measure *up* to the standard. The child's language system initially involves a different system of rules for word combinations.

The child uses a two-word phrase pattern that, although similar to the noun-phrase patterns of adult utterances, serve a number of functions not included in similar adult utterances. If compared to the adult noun-phrase utterance, the child's utterance must be classified as telegraphic speech. It is telegraphic in that it does not contain the articles, adjectives, prepositions, and so forth, in the same manner as a telegram does not. However, while a telegram is a contraction used for expediency, "telegraphic" speech is as complete for the child as an adult sentence is for the adult.

Because the word "telegraphic" does indicate omisson of certain words for efficiency and brevity, the use of that term to describe childhood utterances is inaccurate. McNeill (1970) describes the child's pattern of utterances as containing *pivot* and *open* class words. The pivot class contains a small number of words, each frequently used, whereas the open class contains many more words, each infrequently used. Words from the pivot class tend to appear in combination with words from the open class only, never together. Words from the open class, however, are much more flexible and may appear alone or with each other as well as with words from the pivot class. These two classes of words are complementary.

Most of the research in this area is the result of three major studies: Braine (1963), Brown and Bellugi (1964), and Miller and Erwin (1964). Other research would seem to support their findings. The child develops a word that will serve as a fixing point around which he will build his *sentences.* His sentences will consist of some manner of pivot-open combination. He develops his P-O classifications from the earlier holophrastic utterances. With pivot words used as the core of his sentence formations, the child can develop more and more complex sentences. The open class is further differentiated by a modifier so that the complex sentence contains pivot +open + modifier in various combinations. These modifiers do not as yet contain grammatical units of verb tense or plurals as would be found in adult grammars, but are used as an expansion of P-O grammar. The P-O classification with or without modifiers would not be considered grammatical if used by an adult. It is only when the modifiers are differentiated grammatically that adult units appear. The combinations may occur as follows:

P + O	"my knee"
O + P	"milk allgone"
O + O	"pretty baby"
O	"hot"
P + M + O	"that baby coat"

Morphology

As a child develops more complex phrases, there is a subdivision of the pivot class, like so many layers of skin, until from one class there emerges articles, adjectives, demonstrative pronouns, possessive pronouns, and so on. Braine (1963) observed that second combinations may increase from 14 possible pairs to some 2500 possible pairs in a very short period of time. By this time we can say that the child has the morphological properties of language. Morphology is that part of the language that constitutes the rules for word formation (the shortest linguistic unit or reference-making utterance involving tense, number, case, and person). Berry (1969) classified morphemes as lexical (noun, verb, and adjective) and functional (determiner, propositional, and conjunctive, etc.). These classes can be found in the following states: free (stands alone such as "cat" or "chase") or bound (plurals and past tense endings). "Free" morphemes are used for vocabulary development, whereas "bound" morphemes have a linking function. Morphemes are considered as a part of syntax development since they are often organized into syntactic classes, and because they have a linking function.

McNeill (1970) states that the span of development for grammatical speech occurs between the ages of one and one-half to three and one-half. During that period the child develops a "pivot-open" class system from holophrastic utterances and expands the P-O system. Brown and Bellegui (1964) also state that grammatical development takes place during an approximate eighteen month period from the first appearance of single words to the expansion end of the pivot-open period. Holophrastic utterances, then, have semantic and syntactic properties, while the P-O distinction contains morphologic characteristics as well. The following table is a sample of pivot and open class words. The left hand column contains pivot class words and the right hand column contains open class words. It is not difficult to see that pivot class words are multipurpose and less concrete bound than open class words. Pivot class words have more of a generalizing quality and can be used in a variety of situations.

COMPETENCE VS PERFORMANCE

Table II represents a sample of P-O performance. The combinations of P-O utterances depend on the size of the child's vocabulary as well as the number of his experiences. What researchers have attempted to do in the area of psycholinguistic theory is to predict the probability of performance from vocabulary sample. Performance probability is then used to hypothesize competence level for certain age groups. Competence is the potential knowledge of the speaker and is based on size of vocabulary, internalized rules for phrase-structure, and the speaker's ability to recall these rules on any given occasion. Performance

TABLE II

PIVOT AND OPEN CLASSES: THREE STUDIES OF CHILD LANGUAGE

Braine PIVOT	*Braine* OPEN	*Brown* PIVOT	*Brown* OPEN	*Ervin* PIVOT	*Ervin* OPEN
allgone	boy	my	Adam	this, that	arm, baby, dolly's, pretty, yellow, come, doed
byebye	sock	that	Becky	the, a	other, baby, dolly's, pretty, yellow
big	boat	two	boot	here, there	arm, baby, dolly's, pretty, yellow
more	fan	a	coat		
pretty	milk	the	coffee		
my	plane	big	knee		
see	shoe	green	man		
night-night	vitamins	poor	Mommy		
	hot	wet	nut		
	Mommy	dirty	sock		
	Daddy	fresh	stool		
		pretty	tinker-toy		

Reprinted from David McNeill: Developmental Psycholinguistics. In *The Genesis of Language, A Psycholinguistic Approach,* by Frank Smith and George A. Miller (Eds.), © 1966 by permission of the M.I.T. Press, Cambridge, Massachusetts.

is the expression of competence. It is the skill that the speaker exhibits on any one occasion or number of occasions. Performance is not the infinite range of the speaker's potential. What you do with language on a day-to-day basis is performance. What you have incorporated and internalized into your language system from past experience and the total memory for those experiences, is competence. It is obvious that any researcher will find it difficult to measure a child's (or an adult's) competence as it is only possible then to theorize about competency based on performance probability. In addition, it is extremely difficult to develop such theories about competence based on one contact such as an intelligence or language test. Since most of language is used in reference to specific situations, situational clues and attitudinal sets, a standardized test instrument tends to gather information about surface performance and vocabulary memory rather than overall language competency. "But performance is not a sure measure of the underlying competency, being limited by all kinds of grammatically irrelevant factors, such as restrictions of memory and speaking rate. We are, for example, able to understand much longer written sentences than spoken utterances . . . ." (Hadding-Koch 1969).

Another factor involved in the performance/competency dichotomy is that we know a child's performance is often altered by external stimulation, but we are unsure of the degree influences of external stimulation play on competency. McNeill (1966) reports an exchange between mother and child in which the child resisted the mother's attempts to introduce a new grammatical form although it was obvious that the child understood the message.

Child: Nobody don't like me
Mother: No, say "nobody likes me"
Child: Nobody don't like me

•
•
•

(eight repetitions of this dialogue)

•
•
•

Mother: No, now listen carefully: say "nobody likes me."
Child: Oh! Nobody don't likes me

Smith (1970) attempted to determine how much of what a child receives is judged as grammatical by the child and how much of what he receives becomes incorporated into his speech. She determined that she could not, on the basis of her research, add any information on the organization or semantic value of the messages received by children. It was obvious that children use selective listening in an attempt to process incoming information. The thirteen children in this study experienced more difficulty in repeating grammatical than ungrammatical stimuli.

They also appeared to have some difficulty processing information when an unfamiliar or nonsense word was used as the initial word. Smith concluded that intonation provides the basic cues for the processing of information. Since we place more stress on action and naming words, these words are more frequently incorporated into the child's speech than other words. The child's ability to process information also appears to be determined by the amount of compression of the incoming message. Compression refers to the way semantic information occurs in a sentence. Low compression sentences are easier for the child to repeat. The semantic information of a low compression sentence is distributed evenly. High compression sentences are more difficult for the child with the semantic information bunched at noun-phrase or verb-phrase level containing several information carrying elements. High compression sentences are obviously more adult-like structures.

This research is typical in that it tells us something about the child's ability to repeat information, but it does not clarify how much of that information is used to modify his grammatical structure or competency. We can only surmise that as the child's expressive ability moves from holophrastic utterances to pivot-open utterances to adult phrase-structures, he gains the ability to incode more complex information. This ability is influenced by incoming stimuli but the development of complex grammatical structure is species-specific. We have yet to develop the type of methodology that will measure a child's competency without using performance since a child cannot tell us how he determines grammatic classifications.

LANGUAGE ACQUISITION DEVICES

As the child develops more complicated pivot-open class productions, his level of competency moves from the child's grammatical structure to an adult's system of grammatical structure. This progression is propagated by a number of events. First of all, his experiences demand a more complex categorization of concepts. As his world increases, the number of new experiences provide him with concepts that cannot be handled through holophrastic utterances. For example, negation and question utterances develop as he explores the world. Negation utterances consist of a negative word plus an otherwise affirmative sentence. Questions arise as a result of using rising intonations and/or a few Wh-words (McNeill, 1970).

"Mommy 'no fake–affirmative	"No go byebye?"–negation
"Baby byebye?"–question	"Where 'no fake?"–question

At the same time, the child's utterances are reinforced and expanded through stimulation from his parents (similar to Skinner's description of autoclitic). These reinforcements are couched in the adult's grammatical system. They provide the child with a model for change.

As the pivot-open class becomes more complex, these statements begin to resemble adult speech. Researchers have stated that the child has a "device" (somewhat neurophysiological in nature) that enables him to develop "a theory of regularities that underly the speech to which it has been exposed" (Chomsky, 1957). This device represents his innate competence for language. Surely, man is unique in that he can develop a complex language system in which there is an inherent structure that cannot be totally observed in the actual utterance. The child's knowledge about the development of complex utterances cannot be accounted for totally by environmental stimulation and learning. This device has been termed LAD or Language Acquisition Device, or LAS, Language Acquisition System. McNeill (1970), states that it operates in this fashion:

Corpus ——→ LAD ——→ Grammatical Competence

Corpus would be defined as the "body" of language; that is, all those concepts that the child has uttered and comprehended prior to the development of grammatical competence of the adult's linguistic system. It is a moot question as to whether the child's acquisition of grammatical competence can be described by such a fictionalized device as LAD. This type of theorizing does, however, serve to fill the gap of transition between child and adult linguistic structure. Generative theory (Chomsky, 1957) is a system of rules that can be used to structurally describe sentences of more complex (adult) linguistic units. It is a description of the internalized rules of language intuitively used by an idealized native speaker.

TRANSFORMATIONAL GRAMMAR

When pivot-open class distinctions no longer serve to describe the child's linguistic units, the descriptive methods of generative theory are helpful. Transformational grammar is now commonly used to describe generative theory. This descriptive method implies that there is a universal grammar in which there are rules that generate deep structures together with rules that map these structures into appropriate surface structures (Deese, 1970). These rules can be used to describe all of the sequences of linguistic units that are sentences and all of those that are not.

There are basic rules of language that are universal, such as the use of sounds to develop words and the concept of sentences (Greenberg, 1963). However, the particular grammatical relationships of a language (word order of sentences and relationships of words to each other) are distinctly unique. This uniqueness is referred to as deep structure. Transformation rules effect deep structure by deleting, rearranging and adding elements, such as past tense markers, possessive markers, and so on. At the level of surface structure, appropriate phonological rules are selected and applied to semantic and transformational rules. The end product is what we hear.

In other words, deep structures are those underlying structures that govern how sentences are formed, while surface structures are those sentences that are uttered. The pivot-open distinction of childhood grammar is the base structure (noun-phrase) on which the transformation will ultimately operate (McNeill, 1966). The adult's linguistic unit (surface structure) can be related by transformations to an underlying base structure (Fig. 10).

Sentence - - - - - - - -noun phrase + verb phrase
Noun phrase - - - - - -determiner + noun
Verb phrase - - - - - - -verb + noun phrase
Verb - - - - - - - - - - -denounce, condemn, to be
Noun - - - - - - - - - - -police, student, Lincoln Park
Determinar - - - - - - - -the, in

The surface structure sentence is more efficient, yet it is based on rules inherent in the deep structure sentence. This type of

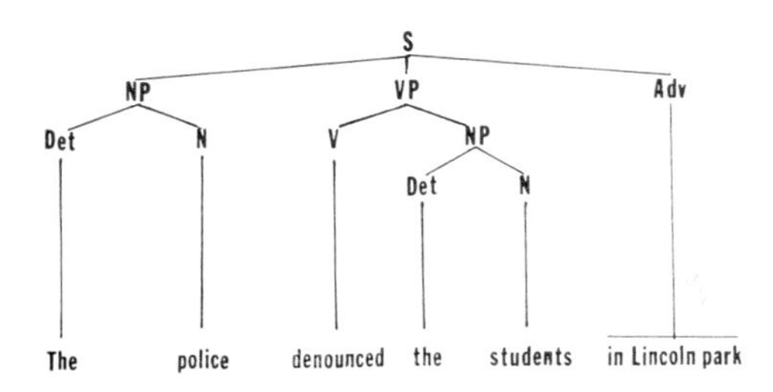

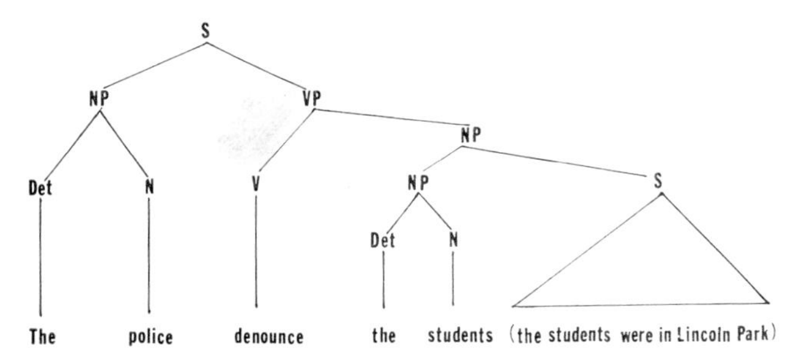

Figure 10. Tree structure of a sentence illustrating transformational grammar model for (a) surface structure, and (b) deep structure descriptions. (From Mansoor Alyeshmerni and Paul Taubr, *Working with Aspects of Language,* © 1970 by Harcourt Brace and Jovanovich, Inc. Reprinted with their permission.)

description serves to let us know how the rules of grammar enable us to develop sentences that are efficient but have an underlying structure based on phrase-unit formation. These rules enable us to make assumptions about those efficient surface units, provide a basis for comprehension, and are the base structures for the formation of new sentences. McNeill (1970) believes that "generative theory tells us that the human mind contains some powerful and general structures for the analysis of language . . . ."

At the risk of offending the staunch linguists, we will confine ourselves to this very brief and general description of transformational grammar and generative theory. Both pivot-open distinctions and transformational grammar are merely abstract methods of describing sentences. Transformation description can be used as a basis for future study of linguistic structures once the child has developed complex utterances.

In summary, speech is the tool for language. The young child learns that sounds, intonation, rate, and rhythm are as important to communication as words. His awareness of speech elements begins in the prelinguistic stage. In other words, before the child has a fundamental awareness of word differences, he becomes aware of sounds and patterns of sounds. "Mama" becomes a first word out of a multitude of sounds because he recognizes, is rewarded for, and uses the repetition more often than others. "No" becomes meaningful as a heavy stress monosyllabic sound pattern (usually followed by negative reinforcement).

It is true than many young children are more ardent vocalizers than they are verbalizers. Children are infamous screamers and criers. Sound and physical activity are often one and the same. Running and screaming are not unusual. This often places stress on the vocalization mechanism, causing some degree of damage. Most children learn without incident, however, to control the articulators and other mechanisms of speech. The child often develops better resonance (quality) and articulation through these intense vocalizations. Although the degree of articulation proficiency may hinder the amount of speech understood by others, it rarely hinders the acquisition of new words.

Words are acquired as they are needed and this need is governed by the number of experiences offered by the environment. Each new experience brings new meaning to previously acquired words or the introduction of a new word. The child initially lives in a world of words in that the *word* carries the message. His word-unit utterances are referred to as holophrastic. "Mama" carries a host of ideas, from "help me," "oh, there you are," to "what is that?" These ideas are conveyed through intonation and inflectional patterns. As the child gains more words, he begins to combine them in phrase structure patterns called pivot-open utterances. "Mama sleep" is an example of such an utterance. As he moves from two to three to four word utterances, he adds modifiers ("Mama sleep now"). Finally, pivot-open distinctions can no longer serve to describe the complex phrases the child uses. Transformational description is one of the methods that can be employed when the child begins to use sentences of adult complexity.

The question concerning the role of external stimulation has not been resolved. Research indicates that the child gains a significant amount of information from the environment. We also know from research that children eventually pattern their phrase structures after the model provided by the environment. The environment cannot, however, control the complexity of his utterances. The child is equipped to handle language involving naming activity long before he can handle language involving temporal information. He can identify and repeat information long before he can resolve complex problems through language. What we have investigated in this chapter is the result, not the process, of phrase utterances. That the development of those utterances is inherent to the human organism, is a foregone conclusion. The structure of that organism needs to be considered before we examine the process of linguistic development. The next chapter will deal with the neurophysiological mechanism of language.

Chapter Four

NEUROPHYSIOLOGICAL DEVELOPMENT

MAN as the highest order of mammals, not only walks upright but communicates. When we begin to describe the marvelous machinery that produces language, we must of necessity consider that this machinery is primarily suited for functions other than language development. Understand that the organism must both receive and send signals before it can be functional. Understand, too, that I am at this point eliminating environmental and psychological factors from the process for expediency's sake. I am also eliminating those functions that are not directly involved in language production.

What, then, is the makeup of the sending and receiving organism? The neurological components of the human organism are the brain, spinal cord, and peripheral nerves. These components are serviced by three interacting systems known as the central nervous system, autonomic nervous system, and endocrine system. The sensory impulses to connect these systems to their neurological components are carried on cables known as the pyramidal, extrapyramidal and cerebellar motor pathways. These cables are in turn serviced by nerve endings known as effectors and receptors.

THE BRAIN

If we compare the electronic computing device to the functions of the brain, we will obtain the following analogy (Strauss and Kephart, 1955):

1. Servomechanisms—feedback control or closed loop system that operates to control the machine of which it is a part, as for example in vision and balance.

2. Homeostasis includes all activities which tend to maintain

the organism's *status quo*; that is, the development of regulating methods which make the variation of the external environment a matter of little moment.

3. Scanning mechanisms serve the task of selecting and bringing into consciousness those perceptions which apply to the situation and are stored in the nervous system by means of memory traces.

The Cortex

The brain (see Fig. 11) is covered with three meningeal layers: dura mater, arachnoid, and pia mater. These layers cover cortical tissue or gray matter (so colored because it is devoid of blood plexuses). There are six layers of cortical tissue containing nerve complexes that stimulate brain activity. The cortex is wrinkled or marked with many depressions and ridges (folding). The deeper depressions are called fissures, the shallow ones are called sulci, and the ridges between are called gyri.

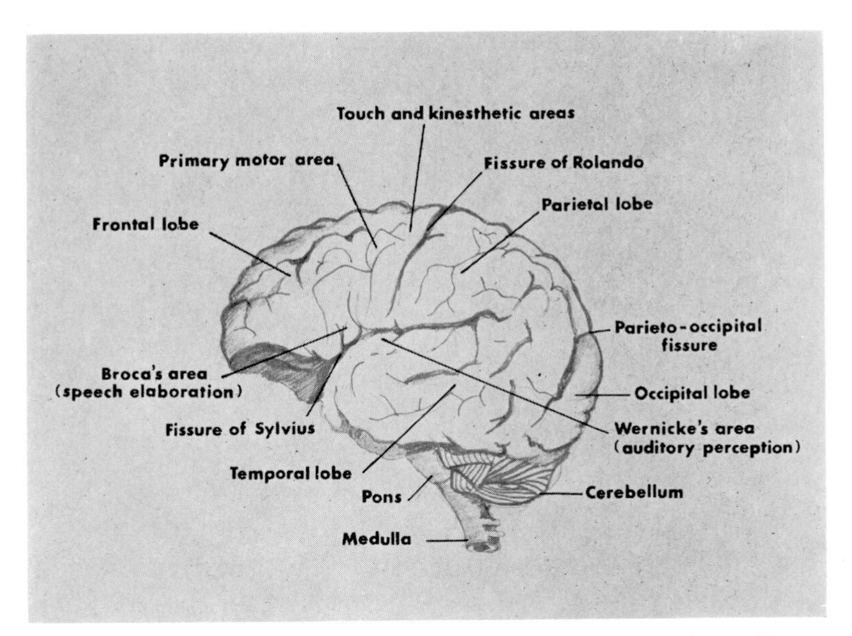

Figure 11. View of left side of adult human brain. (From Giles Wilkenson Gray and Claude Merton Wise, *Bases of Speech*, 3rd ed., 1959, after Watson. By permission of Harper and Row, New York.)

The amount of folding in the cortex serves to indicate the complexity of connections involved in a particular area. Penfield (1964) has stated that a large area of the cortex (eventually involved in language and perception skills) is uncommitted at birth. The activity of the cortex can be measured electronically. Electroencephalographic recordings have given evidence of activity even in the "inert" (or virtually inactive) brain, called *alpha rhythm* (Strauss and Kephart, 1955). The amount of electrical activity of the brain during specific functions (such as speech) has also been measured. The cortex is thought of by some researchers as the final decision maker, receiving its information from the various nuclei through the thalamus. Elliott, (1947) is quoted as saying:

> We may think of the cortex as a huge web suspended between the sensory and motor terminals, . . . as action spreads across the web at every step, it reflects back to the thalamus and receives charges from the thalamus . . . the cortex is analogous to a legislature, the thalamus to a system of committees . . . the relay nuclei to reporters of basic facts of national activity . . . the associational nuclei to the organizers of material who deal with questions arising about the course of action being considered . . . the cerebellum is the civil servant or general staff who reports finished plans and how they have worked.

The Cerebrum

The cortex covers the cerebrum. The cerebrum is divided into hemispheres by the longitudinal fissure, the deepest fissure of the brain. The hemispheres are connected by a bridge known as the corpus callosum. This area is sometimes referred to as the telencephalon. The cerebrum is further divided into four lobes bisected by the fissure of Rolando, the fissure of Sylvius, and the parieto-occipital fissure. These four lobes are the frontal, parietal, occipital, and temporal. For the student of speech and language development there are four major function areas on these lobes that need to be considered. They are as illustrated in Figure 11 (Penfield and Rasmussen, 1950):

1. Sensory terminal—impulses carrying sensory data to and from internal stimuli terminate in a band immediately behind the medial fissure.

2. Motor terminal—impulses carrying motor data to and from internal stimuli terminate in a band immediately in front of the medial fissure.

3. Broca's area—on the third frontal convolution, the speech/motor area, the area concerned with speech expression and designated as area 44.

4. Wernicke's area—on the first temporal convolution, the area concerned with the recognition and interpretation of language, the sensory/auditory center designated as area 22.

The frontal lobe controls muscular movement and thinking. It has been generally recognized that this area has some control over personality and the way in which we relate to the environment. The extent of that control has not been clearly shown through research, but it is evident that after a frontal lobotomy, the patient does not relate to the environment as he did previously although other functions appear to be intact (Gardner, 1942).

The parietal lobe controls sensory discrimination including information about size, shape, and position. It is not visually oriented but proprioceptively oriented. It is concerned with the information used to determine time-space relationships and body orientation. The occipital lobe controls visual relationships and the temporal lobe controls hearing and auditory discrimination. Located forward at the base of the cerebrum is the basal ganglion (part of the telencephalon). It receives and sends out nerve impulses which affect pitch and intonation.

Localization Theory

Most researchers will agree that there is some overlap of function in that one activity requires the involvement of several, if not all, of the cerebral areas and a great deal of the cortex as well. The acceptance of this theory of overall cortical involvement is more widespread among modern day researchers than those of past years. Historically, researchers insisted on a one-to-one relationship between area of function and activity. Researchers who accept the one-to-one relationship thereby are referred to as localizationists.

Although the earliest references to the brain were made thousands of years ago, the localizationist movement began with the studies of brain function conducted in the late 1800's. In 1861, Broca designated the third frontal convolution as the area that controlled motor expression for speech (Travis, 1957). In 1874, Wernicke described the first temporal convolution as the auditory center (Penfield and Roberts, 1959). Bastein further developed the localization viewpoint in 1880 by using diagrams to designate function areas of the brain. This method was later revised and refined by Brodmann whose number classification is still used today (Travis, 1957). Bastein also described the sensory centers for auditory and visual functions. Charcot described the writing center in 1883 and Mills described the motor graphic centers in 1904 (Klingbeil, 1939).

Despite the flurry of activity to locate exact centers of function, there was research to the contrary. Hughlings Jackson, in 1864, was one of the first leading researchers to question the localizationist position (Peise, 1955). He pointed out that their research consisted of autopsies conducted on individuals who had had specific functional deficits. What the autopsy revealed was that there was damage to specific areas of the brain. Jackson stated that knowledge of damaged areas taken from autopsy studies does not define how the area functions in normal individuals. This viewpoint was also shared by Head who in 1926 emphasized that the brain functions as a whole in the performance of tasks (Penfield and Roberts, 1959). Both men agreed that there are areas that are more involved in particular functions but that these areas tend to act in coordination with the entire brain.

Most modern researchers tend to dismiss the localizationist point of view, particularly in connection with language. Weisenberg and McBride (1935), for example, feel that it may be possible to locate relatively fixed areas of control for motion, vision and smelling, but it is relatively impossible to localize such a complex and coordinated function as language. To accept the localizationist theory would be like saying that a burned out light bulb indicates trouble at the power plant. Sugar (1952), among other researchers, has demonstrated that damage to Broca's area does not always result in damage to speech functions. In one instance, he reports the removal of the entire left hemisphere (on which Broca's area is said to reside) without loss to speech function.

Generally, it is held that speech resides on the left side of the brain for right-handed people, and speech disturbances "almost always" occur when the left side is damaged (Sugar, 1952). "Almost always" carries the implication that there is some doubt to this theory. Penfield and Roberts (1959) state that the functional center of the cortex cannot be absolutely localized. Damage has not been proven to be restricted to any specific areas, particularly Broca's. Most of the evidence for the theory of localization is based on autopsy reports, post-morbid condition, and electrical stimulation "aphasic arrest" studies. Furthermore, Mettler and his associates (1949) reported that the removal of Broca's area bilaterally did not result in speech difficulties.

Although electrical activity on the cortex during a particular function can be measured, this measurement may only indicate that this area is *most* involved in the function. What such measurement does not indicate is that an area may need to act in harmony with the entire cortex. Because of the complexity of any language function, it is feasible to assume that the entire cerebral system is involved and not one particular area.

The Cerebellum, Medulla and Pons

Although the cerebrum contains the decision-making areas of the neurological mechanism, it is not the entire mechanism. The cerebellum (part of the metencephalon) is the clearing house for coordinating activity. It is responsible for quick maneuverability during motor activities. It serves to maintain balance through the semicircular canal system and to promote smooth voluntary movement through the cerebellar penducles. The cerebellum modulates motor events and organizes the feedback arrangements of the system. Its relative importance is in the maintenance of motor coordination and in coordinating proprioceptive information about body image and position (Woodburne, 1967). The medulla (part of the metencephalon) controls the rate and depth of respiratory movements. It is more involved in basic regulatory functions but is important in the control of respiration and cardiovascular action during speech.

The pons (part of the myelencephalon) is known as the floating bridge. It is the main bridge between the brain stem and cerebellum. Since the pons is a bridge for motor pathways, it is involved in the motor system. The pons aids in the facilitation and inhibition of basic reflexes. It is involved in respiration and auditory, tactile and kinesthetic discrimination. Along with the reticulm, it is the site of alerting reactions.

The Thalamus

The thalamus, a mass of gray matter at the base of the brain, is part of the diencephalon which receives fibers from all parts of the cortex and is also connected with the covering and fibers of the optic tract. The thalamus (Fig. 12) lies above the midbrain (mesencephalon) medial to the straite bodies, functioning as a sensory relay station. All visual, auditory, somatic, and viseral impulses come through here before going to the cortex. These

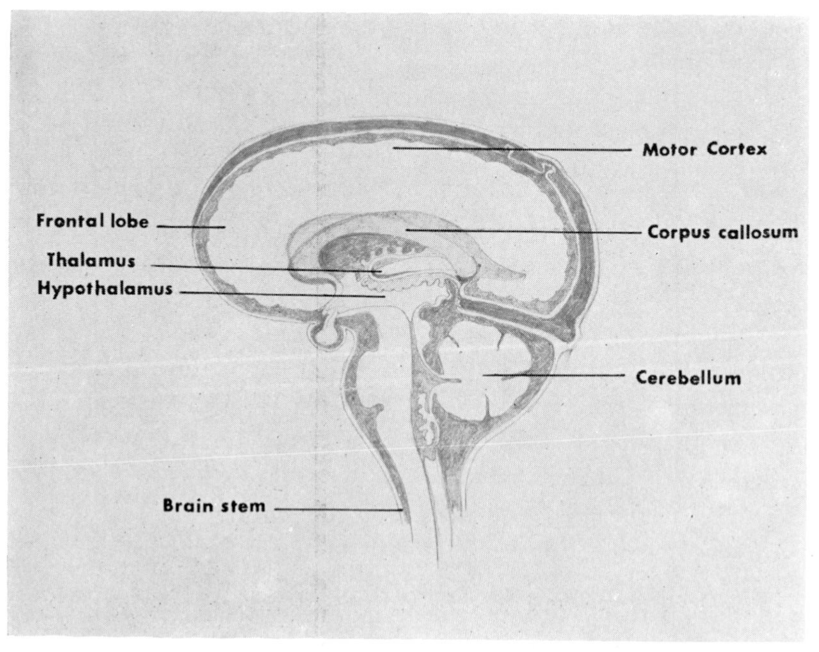

Figure 12. Cross-section view of adult human brain. (Adapted from Plate 21, *The Nervous System,* by Frank H. Netter, M.D. By permission of Harper and Row, New York.)

are the thalamo-cortical and cortico-thalamic pathways (Woodburne, 1967). So direct are the projection pathways from the thalamus to the cortex and from the cortex to the thalamus that its importance as one of the highest integrative mechanisms for speech cannot be ignored. The cortico-thalamic interaction has prompted speculation that the thalamus rather than the cortex controls a great deal of speech function. The basis for this theory is that the thalamus receives all incoming sensations. In addition, all conceptual entities (ideas of form, size, quality, intensity and texture) are organized and presented to the cortex from the thalamus. The thalamus acts as an echoing device between the cortex and itself, and between the motor areas and itself.

The hypothalamus, just below the thalamus, regulates the internal milieu concerning sleep, hunger, pleasure, and displeasure. The hypothalamus acts in conjunction with the pituitary gland to regulate glandular contributions to emotions.

CRANIAL AND SPINAL NERVES

The spinal cord and peripheral nerves must send and receive nerve impulses from the body wall to the brain. There are twelve cranial nerve divisions and thirty-one pairs of spinal nerves. The cranial nerves are as follows (Gardner, 1947):

I. Olfactory—associated with sense of smell, located in olfactory bulb.

II. Oculomotor—five of the seven pair of nerves serving the eye muscles, aid IV and VI (below), originates in mesencephalon.

III. Trochlear—serves single muscle attached to eye aids II and VI, arises from mesencephalon.

IV. Optic—associated with function of sight, forms part of the optic chiasm.

V. Trigeminal—serves muscles of mastication, skin of face and head, mucous membrane of mouth, nasal cavity, located in pons.

VI. Abducent—supplies single muscle of eye along with III and IV, located in pons.

VII. Facial—serves muscles of expression in face, forehead and scalp, at junction of pons and medulla.

VIII. Auditory—associated with sense of hearing and balance, at junction of pons and medulla.

IX. Glossopharyngeal—associated with taste, feel functions of throat, salivary glands and tongue, attached to medulla.

X. Vagus—in conjunction with IX supplies the mucous membrane of the pharynx and larynx.

XI. Spinal Accessory—in conjunction with IX and X associated with muscles of larynx as well as trapezius and sternocleidomastoid muscles.

XII. Hypoglossal—supplies muscles of tongue, located in medulla.

There are thirty-one pairs of spinal nerves: eight cervical in the region of the neck, twelve thoracic in the region of the chest, five lumbar in the region of the loins, and six sacral in the region of the pelvis. These nerves are protected by the spinal column. The functions of the spinal column are as follows: (a) to give stability to the thoracic cage, to permit the body to move in all directions and yet return to a fundamental standing position; (b) to support three structures of considerable weight (head, rib cage, shoulder blades); (c) to provide attachments for numerous flexible bands; and (d) to transmit increasing weight to a fairly inflexible base as well as act as a shock absorber. The most important function of the spinal column is to protect and encase a cord of extreme delicacy. This cord contains the spinal nerves and relays information from the peripheral nerves to the brain. This information is relayed in a coordinated fashion through the use of three systems: endocrine system (ES), autonomic nervous system (ANS), and central nervous system (CNS).

ENDOCRINE SYSTEM

The endocrine system affects its coordinating control in the form of chemical substances called autoacids. These are injected into the bloodstream by secretory tissues of the ductless glands, and serve as stimuli for bodily activity. It is the most basic and closed cycle of the three systems.

AUTONOMIC NERVOUS SYSTEM

The autonomic nervous system is more completely a motor system than the central nervous system. It has an agency for doing things and is concerned with sluggish movements (more visceral) and involuntary movements. It is divided into the parasympathetic system which exerts a restraining and inhibiting influence on glands and plain muscles, and the sympathetic system which exerts exciting and stimulating influences on these glands.

CENTRAL NERVOUS SYSTEM

The central nervous system is an organized agency for knowing things. It is concerned with rapid coordination and voluntary movement. It involves connections between the sense organs and muscles of the body and the nerves of the brain and spinal cord. Motor (efferent) fibers carry impulses away from the CNS; sensory (afferent) fibers carry impulses toward the CNS. The following are differences between the CNS and ANS (Grey and Wise, 1959).

1. Individual fibers of CNS are convered with myelin separating the fibers; the ANS does not have this.
2. CNS as a motor system serves to stimulate the striped muscles of the body (red muscles); the ANS serves to stimulate the secretory tissues (glands and secreting membranes) and plain muscles (white muscles).
3. CNS is capable of rapid coordination; the ANS is confined to sluggish movements.
4. The CNS is more directly under the control of the conscious will than the ANS.
5. The ANS is more completely a motor system than the CNS.
6. The ANS has an agency for doing things while the CNS has an agency for knowing things and is more highly organized set with fibers to the external world.
7. The ANS is divided into parasympathetic (restraining and inhibiting) and sympathetic (exciting and stimulating). The CNS is composed of nerves contained within the cranium and spinal column along with the afferent nerves (connecting brain and spinal cord to sense organs) and efferent nerves (connecting brain and spinal cord to striped muscles of body).

The nerve cable or pathways are the third of the necessary

neurological elements. The pyramidal and extrapyramidal tracts service the motor areas of the cortex and those of the midbrain or mesencephalon while the cerebellar motor pathway services the hindbrain or coordinator (myelencephalon).

PYRAMIDAL TRACT

The most important of these cables or tracts is the pyramidal tract (or corticospinal tract). Its nerve fibers descend downward from the fifth layer of the cortex through the bulb of the midbrain before decussating to the other side to join the nerves of the spinal cord. This final combination eventually controls some of the muscles that produce speech. This cable has a primarily excitatory function involving those messages used to control conscious and voluntary activities of the body. When injured, this control is lost, muscles become spastic and clumsily uncoordinated. This pathway for the nervous impulse must be intact for all the coordinated skills that involve delicacy and precision of movement (Gardner, 1952). These skills would include writing, typing, and speaking. The nerve impulses that travel this cable inhibit random movements and organize purposeful ones. "Just saying the word nuts represents a veritable symphony of nervous impulses arising in the brain and flowing downward to the muscles" (Brown and Van Riper, 1966).

EXTRAPYRAMIDAL TRACT

The extrapyramidal tract is the second major channel. These impulses go downward from the precentral motor cortex. They are mixed and modified by other controlling impulses from the midbrain before joining the terminals of nerves that run outward to the muscles used in speech. Most of the muscles used in speaking are arranged in opposing sets. In opposition to the pyramidal tract, the extrapyramidal tract serves to stabilize actions through relaxation and inhibition (Woodburne, 1967). The simple act of an audible yawn is beautifully and automatically coordinated by such opposing sets of muscles. Nerve impulses descending down the pathway regulate such functions as the pitch, rhythm, and rate of utterance. Sufficient air for speech is also controlled by this pathway.

CEREBELLAR MOTOR PATHWAY

The third major cable, the cerebellar motor pathway, lies behind the midbrain and below the cortex in the cerebellum (hindbrain or birdbrain). Impulses from the cerebellum set the muscles of speech in a state of readiness to contract, coordinating breathing with the movements of the lips and tongue. This set-to-attend mechanism is an essential aid in regulating the flow of speech. It provides the mechanism with feedback loops that further aid in monitoring the flow of speech (Brown and Van Riper, 1966). Thus, when there is damage in this area, speech becomes distorted and uncoordinated. Such speakers sound drunk and disoriented. A local anesthetic from the dentist will induce the same loss of proprioceptive sensation.

OVERALL NEUROLOGICAL FUNCTION

Remember that these pathways are like escalators with descending and ascending fibers so that we can monitor our responses on a feedback system. When we have anesthetized the mouth we are unable to establish adequate feedback and our speech becomes slurred and distorted. There are three degrees of complexity of reflexes that will give us a clue to the level of neurological function under certain conditions (Grey and Wise, 1959):

1. The simplest are very direct involving one efferent and one afferent and one internuncial connection in the spinal cord, medulla, or pons, e.g. bright light—eyes blink, involuntary, requiring no conscious effort.
2. This type of reflex may be prolonged or may be strong enough to cause an additional response in midbrain as well as additional motor neurons, e.g. bright light continued causes shifting of whole body, no experience.
3. Reflexes involving the whole brain or cerebrum, e.g. bright light —shifting body—removing or adjusting light, requires experience.

The following schemata illustrates the relationship of incoming and outgoing sensory/motor pathways to the levels of neurological function. It does not take into account specific areas such as those considered by the localizationists, but is an overall

TABLE III

THE RELATIONSHIPS OF INCOMING AND OUTGOING SENSORY/MOTOR PATHWAYS TO LEVELS OF NEUROLOGICAL FUNCTION

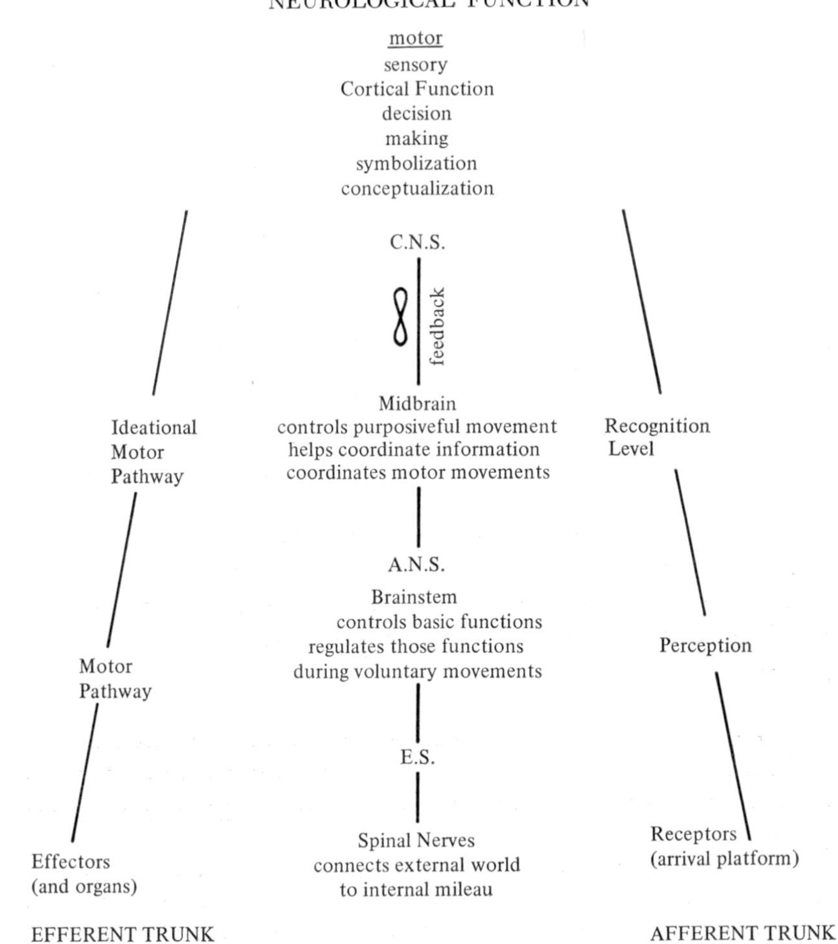

plan for neurological function. It is an adaptation of similar schematas used by Wepman (1960), Osgood (1963), Morely (1965), Karlin (1965), and others.

Using this schemata as a basis, overall neurological function can be summarized in the following manner. The organism is equipped to receive and send information. This information originates internally as well as in the external world. "Simple" functions of the human organism are governed by neurological mechanisms of great complexity. "Higher" functions are governed by neurological mechanisms of greater complexity. Uncomplicated neurological mechanisms do not exist. In the initial stages of life, the neurological system is geared toward the internal milieu. Sleep, hunger, thirst, and comfort are of prime concern. Information about internal milieu is governed by the endocrine system (ES).

Although sensations from the external world are received (receptors), they are attended to only with respect to internal conditions. Later the infant begins to perceive differences in these incoming stimuli (level of perception). He begins to attend to the environment. His waking hours have increased. The motor system becomes more of a conscious system than a reflexive system. At the stage of internal control of activity, he may only blink his eyes when a bright light is introduced. If the light stays on, he may eventually squall with indignation. As he begins to interact more with the environment (and concurrently gain more control of motor activity), he will turn away from the light as well as blink his eyes. This activity is governed by the motor pathway and is an autonomic nervous system (A.N.S.) and brainstem function. Eventually, he will learn to shift his entire body away from the source of irritation. Although he certainly continues to rely on squalls in moments of great stress, he begins to attend to the *results* of his squalls. He is pleased if crying brings mother, but concerned when it brings someone else. If mother does not appear, he may frown and in a few moments resume crying. If mother appears at the sound of the second crying, he may smile.

It is at this point that the infant learns to sort his perceptions (Recognition). Through trial and error, he recognizes those perceptions that yield pleasurable feedback and those that do not. He recognizes a great many things in the environment, including people and objects. He begins to explore the environment. This exploration is at first a motor activity. He discovers his foot and then, a great tool—his hands. He has begun to initiate voluntary motor activity. He can coordinate movements in order to reach his goal (more often than not it is something

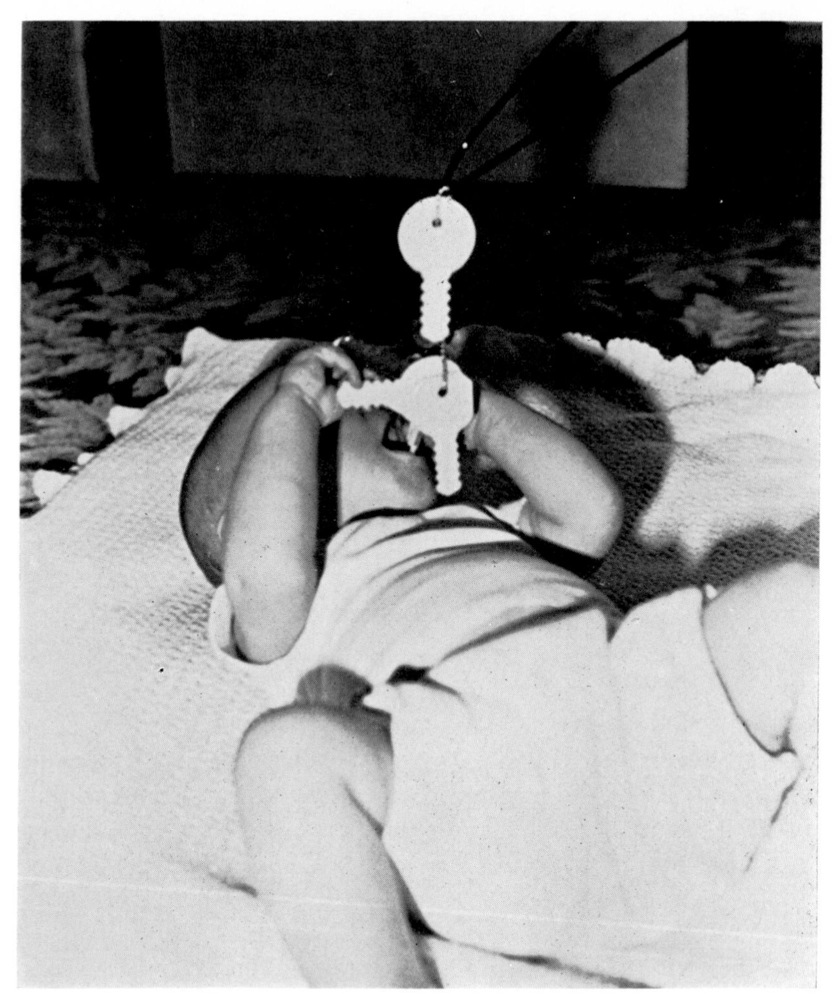

Early motor activity is characterized by an internally controlled reach-grasp-retrieve-mouth cycle. (Courtesy Wood Photographs)

mother would just as soon he did not explore). He has an idea and the motor ability to perform the action. These functions are governed by the ideational motor pathway at the level of the midbrain. Finally, he begins to coordinate motor activity and recognition ability in the area of speech. He becomes a verbal rather than a vocal being. He has made sounds (babbling), but now these sounds become words. He combines motor and sensory information at the cortical level. He not only has ideas, but words. He uses words to express these ideas and solve problems. Thinking is a major activity of cortical level function. We will concern ourselves with the particulars of cognition (thinking) and problem solving in the next chapter.

NEUROLOGICAL DEVELOPMENT

As the previous discussion implies, the neurological system is also governed by developmental schedules. Lenneberg (1966, 1967) states that it begins with the undifferentiated, internally oriented postnatal stage and progresses to the highly coordinated and organized adult stage. At the initial stages of this period of development, the child is limited by the system's immaturity. At the adult level, the individual is limited by an inability to reorganize the system.

Lenneberg states that during the initial periods of neurological maturation (up to 20 weeks) approximately 60 to 70 per cent of CNS development occurs. Each hemisphere has equipotentiality of function. If a lesion (damage from accident or disease) should occur, language is not affected in half of the cases. In the other half, there may be a delay but no permanent damage to language will result. During this period, the child progresses from cooing to babbling. From twenty-one to thirty-six months, language function appears to involve the entire brain. Although the right hemisphere still has a chance to become the dominant hemisphere, the left hemisphere appears to gain dominance toward the end of the twenty-one to thirty-six month period. If there is a lesion, language must be relearned and can be reacquired through a repetition of the stages of normal language development. The rate of maturation of the CNS is reduced and handedness emerges. The child has acquired approximately 200 words by twenty-one months, 400 by twenty-seven months, and 1,000 by thirty-six months. He moves from two to four word P-O utterances.

From three to ten years, adult language structures develop. Grammatical classifications appear and sentence structure becomes more complex. The entire maturational process of the neurological system is sharply reduced in rate. Cerebral dominance is established between three to five years for the left hemisphere although the right hemisphere is still somewhat active. There is, however, a definite polarization of activities for the right and left hemispheres. Recovery from lesions becomes more difficult. Language may be regained but residual disorders of reading and writing may persist. After this period, Lenneberg states that neurological development reaches a level of "plateau." Any lesion causes some permanent damage and language disorder residuals are common. Hemispheric dominance has been firmly established. CNS maturation is, for all intents and purposes, complete.

This is not to say that learning does not take place past this point, but beyond this point, behavior is governed by established patterns of responses. Attitudinal sets have been organized. The acquisition of new methods of handling information and solving problems involves a building of information and solutions along the lines of previously learned techniques, percepts, and attitudes. What we do with a child in grades K-12 cannot be ignored in an institution of higher education since that child has learned to operate in an academic situation only by his personal past experiences.

Perhaps the fault of *innovative* education lies not with new ideas, but with the time for initiating those ideas. The motto for many totalitarian rulers has been, "Give me a boy before he's twelve and then, he's mine." Once a child has developed an organized system of doing things, he continues to use those methods until his attitudinal sets and views of the world have been drastically changed. It should be noted, for example, that a second language becomes extremely difficult after neurological plateau has been reached. If we have not been taught to think in bilingual terms, then monolingual patterns tend to persist.

The important point to remember here is that the young child is in the *process of development.* No aspect of his character should be perceived in stabilized, complex adult terms. The complexity of the child lies in his ever-changing system rather than in the organization and utilization of his abilities. Each day he learns to handle some new aspect of his environment. Each day brings about a change in some area of development. Before we consider the cognitive processes, let us take a look at the second aspect of neurophysiological development, gross motor activity.

MOTORICAL DEVELOPMENT

The initial motor activities of the infant are reflexive. They, too, are geared toward homeostasis. Sucking movements occur soon after birth. It is reasonable to assume that these movements might also occur before birth just as other reflexive motor movements. Most activity during the postnatal period involves generalized movements. The tonic neck reflex and clenched fists posture characterizes early motor involvement. At this point the neurophysiological mechanism is making every attempt to gear itself to life outside the womb. Energy is valuable and is directed toward eating. The baby spends most of his time asleep.

Early Infancy

Some time around the fourth week, the child begins to react to the external world on a limited basis. During early infancy there is no coordination between the eye and hand; however, the ability to follow a moving object with the eyes through an arc of about 90 degrees is developed by the fourth week (Gesell and Armatruda, 1941). Waking activity increases noticeably after this period. Now the infant becomes momentarily concerned with external conditions. Most babies have "learned" that crying brings immediate attention long before this. I say learned only in that crying is his only alternative to discomfort, and mother is perhaps conditioned to the crying, thereby reinforcing it. Certainly crying at this time is no longer as ambient as in the first few weeks of life. There are cries of anger, pain and frustration. The child's family becomes quite adept at cry interpretations and babies can easily become accustomed to the "good" life. So, baby cries, mother runs; baby's cry is reinforced and the baby "learns."

Twelve to Twenty Weeks

By twelve weeks, the child is able to follow the arc of a moving object to 180 degrees (Gesell and Armatruda, 1941). During this period he may make no attempt to touch the object although

The young child soon discovers that his hands are his greatest tools. (Courtesy Wood Photographs)

generalized activity often brings his hand in contact with the object. He has difficulty grasping and if an object is placed in his hands, his fingers may release or tighten without voluntary control on his part. Bruner (1969) states that this action appears to have a midline boundary: "One hand will not cross over the midline to help the other get an object to the mouth or even to get a grasp on it." The baby has begun to hold his head erect and his waking hours have been extended. At this point it is very likely that some members of the family are attempting to determine who he resembles most in the family, and the baby (wide-eyed since he still has some difficulty focusing), coos and gurgles in response. Most of his vocalizations are still internally controlled, but he does begin to respond to tone of voice. He will drool an appropriate smile and "recognize" mother.

By the age of twenty weeks, a child can be expected to have developed sufficient eye-hand coordination to see and touch an object placed before him. The first attempts have been unsuccessful. Prior to this period, he may reach and stare at the object for about five seconds, but cannot successfully grasp it. At this level, visually directed reaching emerges (White, 1969). He learns to pull the object toward his body or the other hand, in preparation usually for a taste-test. (Mothers learn to watch earrings and glasses; fathers learn to unknot ties).

The first attempts to reach for an object may involve the "backhand" approach in which the child first touches the object with the back of the hand, then opens the fingers just as his hand moves past to clutch the object (Gesell and Ilg, 1949). The "circuitous" approach or the palmar scoop is also used. It involves a circular motion, but it is of a forward nature. The second approach is considered somewhat more mature than the former one. Grasp attempts are called the "primitive squeeze" at this stage, in which the thumb extends between the middle and forefinger or the middle and ring fingers. Since the child has rarely developed social amenities by this age, feeding time can be a real "squeeze." This is further complicated by his aim. Although most objects are directed toward the taste-test center, body image has not clearly developed, so the mouth is elusive. It is sometimes near the ears, nose, or hair. It will be some time before his aim is perfected (and by this time, mother's track record for reaching his hand before it reaches his mouth has improved).

Body posture also changes during this reaching process. At first, reaching is dominated by the shoulder; after that (in sequential order), the elbow, the wrist and the fingers (Gesell, 1940). Simultaneously, he gains control of the body and begins to sit. It is well to note that the baby does a great deal of practicing at all stages of development. Dropping toys over the edge of the crib is practice of grasp and reach techniques. During this time, the baby appears to be experimenting with various types of grasps, all of them awkward and frustrating versions of the squeeze grasp.

Six to Twelve Months

By the time he is a year old, the child has developed the ability to grip an object between the fingers and thumb which is called the "pincer movement," and hold it without resting his arm on the table or crib rail (Gesell and Armatruda, 1941). Simultaneously, he develops the "straight hand approach" in reaching. The arm is controlled and aimed at the object by the wrist and fingers. He is crawling by this stage, and if he is not taking his first steps, they will soon follow. He can stand and his point of focus has expanded from mother's arm to the floor and the limits of the room. Unless closely watched, the focal point extends as far as he can crawl, hobble or toddle. The child is considered ambulatory and armed. He is in the process of developing verbal skills, but his physical limits have expanded so rapidly that his vocal abilities may appear to have decreased somewhat. Although his ability to *perform* verbal skills may appear limited, he is in the process of developing preverbal skills that will be essential to his later verbalizations. His activity during this sensorimotor period will be discussed later in Chapter Six.

Complete development of motor activity will not occur for another four years or so. At that stage, the child will be able to run and skip as well as walk. His balance improves enough so that he can manipulate toys such as a tricycle or wagon. His grasp improves enough to pour as well as drink or eat with a fork. He will continue to have difficulty with some finer motor movements until he is in the primary grades. Such activities as cutting and tying occur long after he has gained the facility to handle a crayon and use other items requiring small circular and highly coordinated movements. Mothers are often conditioned by children. Many mothers are "toilet trained" by the time the child is a year old, and youngsters know there is more than one way to get dressed even if you *are* four. In any observation of childhood behavior, it is important to remember that gross and finer motor functions as well as speech and language functions operate under a series of well-circumscribed events. One set of functions, however, is not necessarily delayed by the failure of the other to appear. Often motor experimentation precedes language experimentation, or vice versa, although the developmental periods of both the speech and motor areas often seem to coincide.

MATURATIONAL STUDY

Gesell (1940) and Gesell and Armatruda (1941) have observed the patterns of behavior for children during block building activities. Gesell placed nine blocks in a square and a tenth block in the middle of the square. It was observed that the very young child may do no more than touch a block, try to pick it up, or disregard it, at less than one year of age. By the time he is one year old, however, he is likely to want to place blocks next to each other. His play activity has little pattern to it. He is on the floor and stays there, returning to the floor with the blocks when he does decide to play with them. At fifteen months he insists on standing, attending to the blocks for a short time only. He is more involved in generalized gross motor behavior than in finer motor activity. His attention span is extremely short and he may be disturbed by the absence of his mother. At eighteen months, he may accept a chair. He handles the blocks randomly and may scatter them. At two years, he seats himself and remains seated. He builds a tower or puts the blocks in a row. Some children are still inclined to throw them on the floor, but will usually not join them there. He may talk to you for a period of time, but you will probably gain very little information about his activity.

At three, he arranges the blocks horizontally and only occasionally builds a spontaneous tower. His performance is more rigid and he is prone to imitate the movements of a toy such as a train. At four years, the child builds a complicated structure. He may extend it vertically and laterally and give the structure a name. He is more inclined to fantasize in detail about his structure. The five-year-old builds a three-dimensional structure, usually calling it a "house" but often he is inventive in naming it; whereas, the six-year-old reverts to the two-dimensional structure and constructs in terms of the limitations of the material. He will give you any number of suggestions on the limitations and rules of blockbuilding.

These norms, of course, are limited by children who do not

"read the book" and are not aware of researched expectations. They are also limited by children who have not experimented with blocks beforehand and who have difficulty adjusting to new situations. Most motor-behavior norms are more valid when offered by the realistic parent. It would seem, however, that most children tend to perform in the manner described in this section, at least by sequence, if not by schedule.

The neurophysiological mechanism enables the child to explore his world. Through these explorations he gains perceptual and sensory information that will aid him in linguistic coding activities. The child does not arrive in this world with an awareness of the "world." He does not even arrive with the ability to cope with the world. It has often been said that the human infant is the most helpless of all newborn creatures. In a span of three years, this very helpless creature will begin to out-think and, more importantly, out-talk any animal of the same age who might lay claim to superiority in these areas.

The child owes a great deal of his ability to his second greatest tool, his hand. First and foremost, however, he is able to perform all of these marvelous activities as the result of his greatest tool, a complex neurological mechanism. In the next chapter, we will explore the highest level of neurological function, cognition. Thinking is a cortical level function, but the information brought to this level depends on the child's ability to coordinate cortical function with the activity of the entire neurophysiological mechanism.

Chapter Five

LANGUAGE AND COGNITION

ALTHOUGH normal development of speech depends upon the functional integrity of the neurophysiological mechanism, it also depends on a stimulating and rewarding environment. Language is initiated before verbal skills are apparent. These preverbal skills are developed through sensorimotor expression in infancy. The infant's initial sensorimotor manipulations are untaught. His experiences enable him to use these manipulations in later developmental stages for more complex functions, such as language. These experiences must provide him with reinforcement for his manipulations as well as allow for growth through experimentation.

EGOCENTRIC BEHAVIOR

The child's attitude toward a particular task must be one that will not hinder his performance. He must feel that he can experiment on a risk-free basis without losing self-esteem. The responses of the people in the environment toward his past ability to perform tasks, as well as their attitude toward the initiation of a new task, must be favorable.

Let us return to motor skills for a moment to clarify this point. By the time the child is ambulatory, his world begins to expand rapidly each day. His need to explore that world also expands, as does his need to gain independence. He has developed the straight hand approach and the pincer grasp, but he is not efficient in using them. This rarely slows him down. He will attempt pouring and pulling activities until he becomes proficient at them; that is, unless his experimentations are halted by mother. Parents are naturally, and logically, protective of the young child. Quite often, however, this leads to hesitancies on the part of the youngster. "Junior" is not allowed to pour milk because he is clumsy. Junior knows this (he's been told enough), so he hesitates just prior to the attempt and, usually, spills the milk. Junior needs to develop pouring skills *and* cleaning skills. In this way, he learns the circular movements involved in cleaning and gains some satisfaction from the pouring attempt. His experimentation attempts have also been reinforced under supervised conditions.

No task can be successfully performed unless the child is ready for it and is appropriately stimulated for the experience. This is not to imply that there is a mode or standard of stimulation. It does imply that the child needs to find some point of reference between the environment and the act, and that he is somehow rewarded for the attempt. Motor and adaptive activity are intimately linked. Adaptive refers to the appropriateness of behavior in accordance with the specific situation and social restrictions of the culture. Adaptive behavior is closely related to intelligence, for intelligence is the capacity to initiate *new* experiences and profit by the experiences thus initiated. The infant's inquisitiveness and manipulations are untaught. They also determine what and when he will learn through reinforced experiences.

The child's behavior sums up his reactions to other persons in the culture. So great is his sensitivity to his perceptions that it may, at times, seem to be in advance of his awareness of his own manipulations. His ability to relate to the experiences of others appears to be an "honest" cruelty. This lack of empathy colors all of his experiences. The world of things and the world of people are virtually blended for the infant. He often reacts to how mother handles his toys with the same intensity of emotions displayed at breakfast earlier in the day. It appears impossible for him to separate himself from his surroundings. He and the world are one.

Piaget refers to this as *egocentricism* (Piaget, 1959). The child uses speech to bring order to his world. He uses speech to confirm his investigations and to seek information. Piaget explains that egocentric speech is not entirely socialized speech. The child does not place himself in the point of view of the listener. This may explain, in part, the "cruel" honesty of children. The inquisitive nature of his speech is so strong that he may rely on no more than apparent interest in his verbal activity. His initial verbalizations are egocentrically oriented (Piaget, in Hall, 1970). Very often this lack of priority between things and people leads to frustration and irritation, just as it leads to the need to express ownership and opinion.

Vygotsky (1962) stated that egocentric speech patterns help orient the child toward the world. The child, at first, cannot differentiate speech for himself from speech for others. Eventually this egocentric speech behavior helps him make the transition from verbal speech to silent thought. He internalizes these speech patterns and develops inner speech. He no longer thinks out loud. Egocentric speech, then, helps him establish himself in the scheme of things.

Part of the task of language is that it helps the child establish verity. He will say, for example, "cup broke?" at the sound of a broken cup in order to confirm his own suspicions. It also helps him establish his own validity. It is not uncommon to overhear a mischievous youngster, during the very act of mischief, say, "no, no, bad boy." Part of the task of language development is to achieve distinction between the infant and others. For example, I waited anxiously for the first word phrase of my second child. Since my first child was a highly verbal youngster, I expected almost anything as a result of his promptings. We were both astonished when "leave me alone, boy" tumbled forth one day. The need to achieve individuality had prompted a multiple word phrase, not vice versa. The progress of preverbal and verbal responses are decisively influenced by the culture and the environment of the child. In addition, these responses are subject to the laws of language and cognitive development.

COGNITION

"Even though we spend much of our lives with other people, most of our conversation is silent—in self-communication, in thought" (Brown and Van Riper, 1966). The child makes the most important tool of all, symbols, which will serve as a catalog of his perceptions. His initial egocentric utterances are of three main types: interjections, denominations (naming activity), and commands (Church, 1961). Interjections are pivot words such as "bye bye." When the child learns to manipulate these symbols and conceptualize ideas, he is thinking. There seems to be an all-powerful urge to create those symbols.

Determining Tendency

Thinking is making and manipulating analogies, comparing similar but unique things, and creating new combinations of symbols whenever we encounter an experience for which we have no name (Brown and VanRiper, 1966). Although we think in both verbal and/or picture symbols, we tend to create a verbal mental image for those experiences that are the result of several events. For example, "bread" and "running" may be pictorial, whereas "disorder" and "goal" are verbal. In all thinking, however, there seems to be a need to create a symbolic pattern. This has been referred to as *determining tendency* (Brown and VanRiper, 1966). We need a word for "it," otherwise our world becomes chaotic. The infant can be observed in this stage when he attempts to place a new word on many objects. He finally discovers that "ball" does not include "orange" or "egg" although both are essentially shaped in the same way. This does not mean that he automatically has the word for "orange." He must eat the orange, smash the orange, lose the orange, drink orange juice, etc., before he encompasses the concept of "orange." There must be a downward classification of the concept. "The newly acquired ability to know things that are present is soon followed in the two-year-old child by the ability to represent that which is known" (Furth, 1969).

Cognitive Dissonance

Later, the child will begin to make assumptions about symbols prior to the development of the symbol. This is known as *cognitive dissonance* (Festinger, 1957). It is the development of assumptions and anticipations prior to the formation of symbols for new ideas. Church (1961) stated that "children are largely immune to cognitive dissonance, as seen in their insensitivity to contraditions, paradoxes, and logical (as oppossed to factual or moral) inconsistencies." In other words, cognitive dissonance does not occur until attitudinal sets have begun to develop. There must be preconceived notions prior to the development of ideas and in the child's world of "Wonderland" such notions rarely exist, all things are possible. Perhaps the foundations for cognitive dissonance lies in the development of emotions as a viable means of relating to the world. As the child becomes less egocentric, he develops a different emotional perspective. We learn to react to people and things long before we learn to identify on an objective basis. "Meanings precede objects in perception" (Church, 1961). We attend to those perceptions that have become important to us; those perceptions that we are accustomed to using in the development of symbols. The child eventually learns to differentiate the important perceptions through his past (emotional) experiences.

Symbolic Association

Symbolic meaning occurs when words can be used in a functional manner. We do not develop symbolic meaning with the introduction of a new word, but only as we find that that word can serve specific functions for us. We manipulate our symbols in a multitude of combinations until we develop language that is appropriately self-satisfying. Piaget (Furth, 1969) stated that this exploration of associations is the second stage of thinking (associations of symbols) occurring between the ages of two to seven. The child manipulates symbols by first repeating the word in a number of situations, or generalizing. He then categorizes his generalizations. These categorizations occur through two methods, upward and downward categorizations (Church, 1961). First, the child refers to all four-legged creatures as dog, or he generalizes. A child who finally recognizes that the horse is not a dog (and yet, not a cow) has made a downward categorization. By adding horse and cow as distinctly different symbols to his knowledge of four-legged creatures, he has expanded his knowledge of similar things. When the child recognizes that there are different kinds of horses and different kinds of dogs but that the two groups are distinctly different, he has collectively classed in an upward categorization. Upward categorizations appear later in the development of categories and require abstraction or the isolation of a single property from the totality of the object. Categorizing all horses together in a class by themselves as opposed to categorizing horses and dogs in a class-four-legged, requires attending to much more discrete perceptual information.

The child learns through verbalization about the structure of the physical world.

> He learns that a balloon and watermelon are the same size, but different in weight; the same or different in color; and quite dissimilar in taste. Thus, he abstracts characteristics and sees things in a combination of characteristics. This symbolic manipulation leads to the power to conceptualize so that even a very young child can understand the symbolic equivalence when he sees the earth among the planets on a television screen, or a horse in a book or himself in a looking glass. He no longer tries to pick up shadows and streaks of light. He learns that beads separated over the length of string do

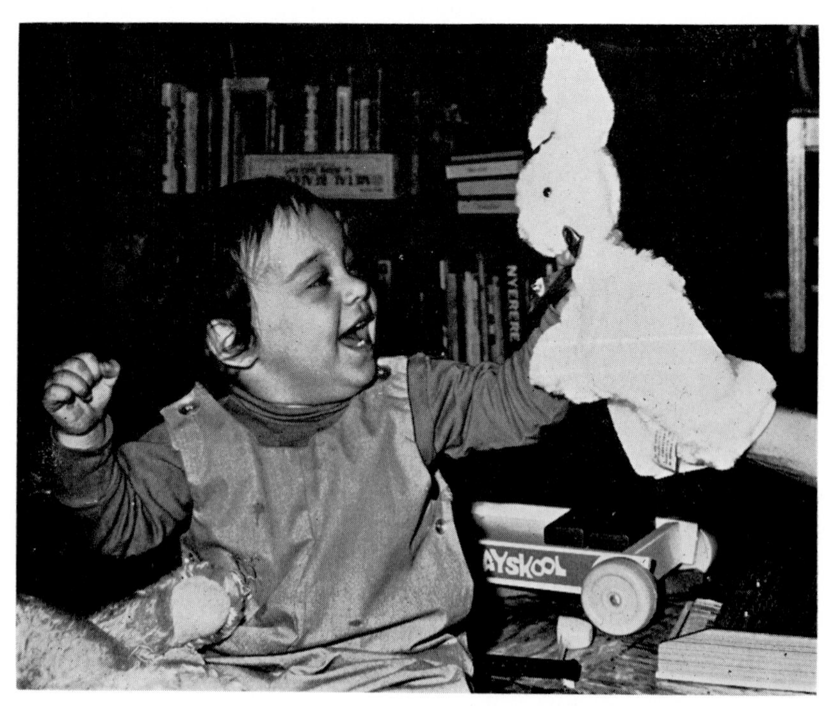

All things are equally real and delightful in a child's world of fact and fantasy. (Courtesy Wood Photographs)

> not make more beads than they do when pushed together. Pushing them together, he throws up his hands and says "See!" (Brown and Van Riper, 1960).

He begins the process of developing structural relationships. He observes the characteristics of things (objects and actions) and begins to classify on the basis of those characteristics. His verbal behavior is indicative of this classification ability.

Patterning

The next stage of thinking complexity is *patterning*. Patterning is placing form on the factual information of inner language or thought. It is really the core of what is referred to as meaning. When we say, "Oh, I see!" what was previously scrambled information now makes sense (Brown and Van Riper, 1966). First, the child explores and symbolizes the environment, he then classifies through symbolic associations, and finally, he categorizes his associations. This final stage involves a more complex system of relationships and interrelationships. Piaget observed that the development of patterning ability constituted the portion of the cognitive process in the years between seven and puberty (Furth, 1969). He called this stage the development of concrete operational thinking. The child categorizes through similarity, negation, and reciprocity. Similarity classifications are expanded from the previous stage. Negation (dissimilar dimensions) and reciprocity (relative relationships) are now utilized. Right-left are negative but maintain a relative relationship to before-behind.

The child has developed the capacity to think about objects when the objects were not present to be manipulated: "If I send for this glow-in-the-dark ring, I'll be a spy." He still fantasizes, but now he is able to manipulate these fantasies with a great deal more facility. It is the stuff box-tops are made of.

The child's language has begun to be more symbolic than signal. He has gone beyond the family pet. For example, the plate stands for food to a dog, and the door stands for going out. But the animal is virtually powerless away from the physical presence of the objects he uses for symbolization (Brown and Van Riper, 1966). He cannot discuss the possibility of weather conditions nor can he discuss the price of food. The child has reached the stage where he is able to develop and manipulate language structures.

Reality Testing

When we think, we manipulate these symbols we have developed in some sort of organized fashion. We attempt to impose order on chaos and check fact and fantasy. This checking process is called *reality testing.* It is the continual reassessment of the world and an attempt toward logic. The child begins reality testing through role play and continues it through linguistic manipulation. Role play is the child's method of exploring the world and its limits. As they play each part, they say different things to fit the role. They assess, through imitation, the role of mother, doctor, teacher. Later these roles will be reassessed verbally. Piaget described this as the stage when the adolescent is capable of forming hypotheses and deducing possible consequences from them (Furth, 1969).

Although reality testing completes the thought cycle, it does not insure growth. The child's role playing is imitative, so he can only operate within the limits of the known world. Later, his reassessments are built on his past experiences with the limitations of his world. If he is to expand his world, he must talk to different people under many different circumstances.

The most basic process to this exploration of the world's limitations is called close identification. Identification is one of the most significant and imaginative linguistic acts. It is the first step in understanding another person. It is what we call "empathy." In other words, we escape the restrictions of self to some extent and consciously imagine what it must feel like to be the other person (Brown and Van Riper, 1966). In a culture in which there are rigid rules of behavior, close identification rarely occurs and the child is restricted to play the roles of only those people who are most like him. Language that involves the self and others serves as a compass letting us know our position in the world in relation to others. Again, a child cannot realize his self-potential unless he is permitted to experiment on a risk-free basis. The approval of others is a powerful force and if that approval does not extend to close identification with roles outside the immediate environment, the child's awareness of the world is limited. He must be provided with the necessary attitudinal sets before this period that will allow such experimentation. Rigidity and bias or acceptance and flexibility begin during the preverbal period.

Cognitive Development (Piagetian Approach)

Before we move to another theory of language development, let us summarize this Piagetian approach to cognition and language through the following schemata. This schemata is also similar to those used by Wepman (1960), Osgood (1963), and Morley (1965).

TABLE IV
DEVELOPMENT OF COGNITIVE PROCESSES UTILIZING THE PIAGETIAN APPROACH

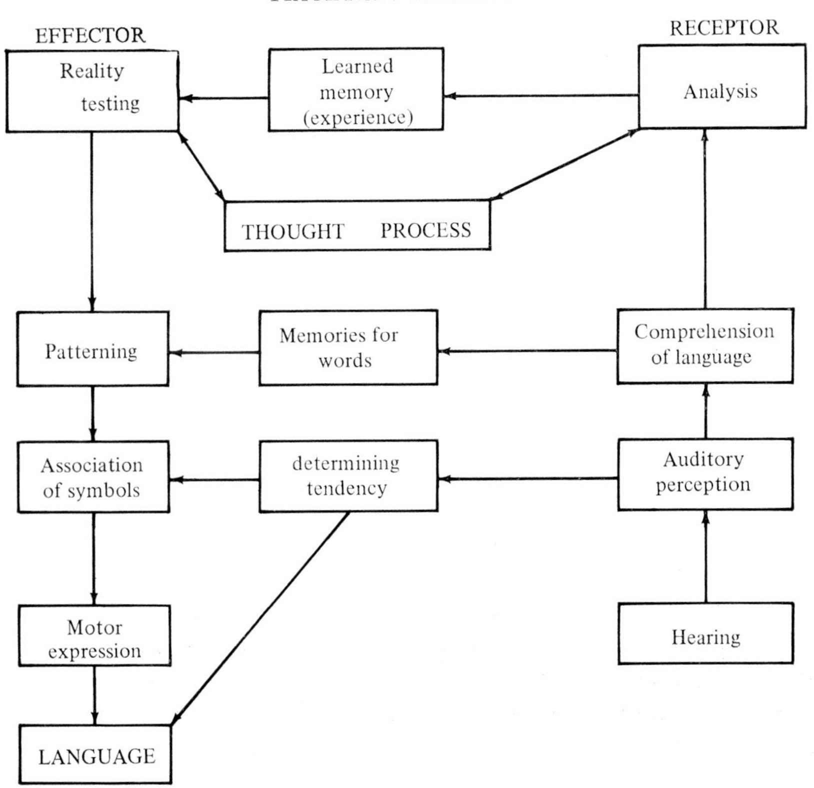

The first stage of cognitive development is a language prerequisite—hearing. The child must be able to receive sounds adequately. This is the arrival platform. The next cognitive stage is perception. The child must be able to perceive that some sounds are different from other sounds. In a previous chapter, auditorization was discussed. It is at this stage (but during a later period), that the child must learn to audit his production as well as the stimulation of others, in order to become proficient in the production of sounds that are contained in his native language.

Once the child is aware of his ability to manipulate the articulators to produce sounds, he begins to develop words as he needs them and as fast as his experiences will allow. This occurs some time during ten to fourteen months. He needs words to make order out of chaos. Soon he will begin to associate these words with other words in order to form categories and comparisons. Simultaneously, he understands more language than previously. His comprehension for language improves. This is a receptive function, but must occur at about the same time as the expressive function, association of symbols. He develops two-word phrases. This skill develops during the second twelve months of life.

From ages two through seven, he begins to store words and ideas. He is full of questions (some of them almost unanswerable, such as "How high is up?"). He fantasizes and is involved in role playing. He still believes in most anything and will question anything. During this period, attention and memory are the most important skills. He learns to observe and to listen as well as to verbalize. Listening is facilitated by clarity and simplicity. The environment must provide him with a choice of simple words that can be easily organized and translated. The answer to "How high is up?" can be "Farther than any man has ever gone," or "Right up to the top of the sky." The young child needs those answers that will give him immediate information without necessarily raising a dozen other questions. It is at this stage that attitudinal sets are begun.

Soon he will begin to use those answers he has stored to solve problems. He will recognize that the "top of the sky" doesn't really answer questions about the limits of height, but he will also recognize that that is a reasonable answer until such time as man goes beyond the moon. He begins to abstract characteristics and distinctions that will help him solve his *own* problems. He uses the attitudinal sets already initiated to discover the world. This is the receptive stage of analysis. It closely follows the patterning stage. He stores those solutions that seem to fit several situations and uses them selectively for future situations.

Well after the age of seven, when the child has some experience in analysis and patterning, he will begin to create theoretical situations, or reality testing. He will learn to manipulate known facts in order to arrive at theoretical solutions. He will use attitudinal sets to evaluate the world as good, bad, or indifferent. While reading this book, for example, you are manipulating familiar facts with new ones in order to arrive at hypothetical solutions. The process of education *should* rest on reality testing; unfortunately, however, most formal education relies on the storage of comprehended language that is scheduled for regurgitation during exams.

Notice that the description of linguistic development used here is sequential. The child need not evaluate symbols at the early stages of language learning in order to produce utterances. Indeed, he may parrot words as the schemata indicates: he hears, perceives, has the word, utters the word. Adults use this "short-cut" also, in that some of our responses are automatic. If we pass someone while in a hurry, we may reply "Fine" to a "How are you?" when, in effect, we are under terrible stress and have a rotten cold. Not all utterances require the complete linguistic process, but the adult language system involves the use of this process.

SERVOMECHANISM THEORY

Another theory of language development is one proposed by Mysak (1961, 1966). Much of what he theorizes is based somewhat on Mowrer's *Autism theory* (1960), and Penfield's *Association theory* (1959). Mowrer states that certain sounds or word-noises may be elicited by the following events:

1. Speaker comes to represent positive emotional connotations for the child, representing pleasant experiences.
2. Speaker produces specific word-noise just before and as he confronts the child.
3. Speaker eventually evokes positive emotional feelings within the child by his word-noise alone.
4. Child experiences positive emotional feedback when he approximates speaker's word-noise during random vocalization.
5. Child repeats approximation and strives to perfect it because of positive emotional feedback.
6. Child retains the learned word-noise because of the influence of social approval.

It is obvious that this is more of a stimulus-response-reward cycle than the previously mentioned developmental sequence. The child hears something, repeats it, and is rewarded. This positive reinforcement causes the child to alter his productions until he has approximated the adult's utterance. He retains those utterances that are positively reinforced.

Penfield's Association theory also influences Mysak's hypothesis. Penfield explains that oral language development is neurophysiological in nature and is formed as the result of three types of neuronal patterns called conceptual, sound, and verbal units. The child conceptualizes an object, hears the sound associated with the object, and verbalizes that sound. This theory is based on the neurophysiological structure of the organism. There is always a one-to-one relationship between sound and object. The establishment of language is cortico-thalamic. What we do with language is the result of neuronal units originating in the central nervous system and eventually stabilized in the speech area of the left hemisphere. Speech is a neurological reflex action.

Mysak utilizes both these theories to some degree. His approach is known as the servomechanism or feedback principle. It places the responsibility for the development of speech on the child's ability to use his feedback or auditing apparatus. The extent of speech development is limited only by the child's ability to utilize incoming speech information supplied by both himself and the environment.

Mysak states that oral language development is the result of simultaneous maturation of the (a) perceptorium, (b) vocalization mechanism, and (c) general motorium development. The perceptorium basically represents an eye-ear-hand unit. It is a visual-auditory-tactual receiver or environmental explorer unit which develops the capacity to integrate (simultaneously) various types of stimuli. These stimuli then represent a new total sensory configuration of some particular part of the child's experience. The vocalization mechanism comprises the respiratory-phonatory-articulatory complex. General motorium (gross motor) development occurs concurrently with development of the perceptorium.

Understand that the servo or feedback theory says that as we talk, information is being fed back into the brain by way of circuits known as closed or open cycles. Our errors are corrected through these circuits. The automaticity of speech requires that these circuits operate in a closely organized process.

The closed circuit or cycle occurs during that period when the child responds primarily to introceptive sensations related to hunger, thirst and so forth. It is a circuit contained within the individual and audits what he says kinesthetically, tactually and auditorially. But most important to us, it is the first cycle on the developmental scale and is related to the basic biological needs of the individual. Primary cycle in this developmental theory refers to the period of feedback of nonpropositional sounds. Propositional speech is that speech which is intended to influence or control the environment. During the primary closed cycle then, the child is involved in introceptive sensations and uses nonpropositional sounds. This is traditionally referred to as the babbling period.

Open cycle is defined as that period in which the child uses sound for the specific purpose of attracting attention. He is then influenced by external components or listener reactions. During the primary open and closed cycle, the child has a few words but is still basically attuned to introceptive sensations and continues to exhibit babbling behavior. In addition, he is echoic in that he can be easily stimulated by external sound sources. He is beginning to attend to the environment.

The next level of development marks the emergence of prop-

TABLE V

SERVOMECHANISM DEVELOPMENT

	Age	*Visual*	*Tactile*	*Auditory*	*Motor*	*Speech*	*Cycle*
System Equilibrium	6/7 weeks 6 months	regard object midline follow to 180°	grasping pulling clutching scratching raking	localizes sound discriminate gross sounds	hold head erect sits scoots	crying cooing gurgles reacts to pleasure by vocalizing	closed: reacts to sound, differ- entiated cries
Primary Closed Cycle Vocalization	6 to 9 months	discriminates individuals	slap and scissors grasp	meaningful motor be- havior responds to name	sit crawl	babbling more consistent	closed: initia- tion of sound for specific purpose
Primary Closed and Open Cycle Vocalization	9 to 12 months	begins eye- hand activity	hitting pushing waving pincer grasp	responds to name, no, other single words	stands, may be walking	echolalia first word	primary open
Closed and Open Cycle Propositional Vocalization	12 to 18 months	recognizes picture	scribble feed self	follow simple directions	walk pushes or pulls toy	single words used meaning- fully	open and closed proposi- tional

Closed Cycle Verbalize	3 years	Child, with aid of speech, stabilizes-expands and maintains an organized sequence of his perceptions; word-noise represents object.	percept formation egocentric language, gestures mimic	closed perceptual linguistic devel- opment
Closed Initial Open Cycle Verbalize	3 to 5 years	Elaborates his own speech by listening, speech is characterized by criticism, requests, questions and answers.	mature attempts at communication shares perceptions	
Closed and Open Cycle Verbalize	7 to 8 years	The perception is no longer limited to a representation of the object experienced, resembles adult symbolic communication.		

ositional speech. The child is oriented toward verbal production. He continues to rely on pleasurable internal stimulation; however, he has now moved into the period where he uses single words meaningfully based on positive reinforcement from the environment. Finally, the child becomes totally propositional. He continues to rely on perceptual information for a period of time, but he has begun to use language as a way of stabilizing his perceptions. He has reached the stage where he will begin to move from vocalization (the utterance of sounds) to verbalization (the use of words). In the final stage of the servomechanism theory, the child has developed a language system that is adult-like. He uses his verbalizations in problem solving and is in the initial stages of logical thinking.

What Mysak proposes is that the child learns language by listening. Mysak places emphasis on the child's use of receptive abilities in the development of expressive language. This theory serves to emphasize the necessity of understanding the use of decoded information before assumptions are made about encoded (expressive) information. One cannot use sentence structure and phrase utterance as the sole means of determining language development. What the child does with what he sees, hears, and feels, *produces* what he says. A look at sentence structure will only serve to give you a sample of the results of all that incoming information.

Regardless of whether you prefer to use the servomechanism approach or the Piagetian oriented theory of cognitive development, it is important to recognize that the child must have the cognitive equipment necessary for the development of speech. He must also be provided with experiences that will stimulate and reinforce cognitive development. The next chapter will be concerned with the psychosocial experiences necessary for speech and how they are guided and shaped by the parents and culture.

Chapter Six

PSYCHOSOCIAL PERCEPTION

DESPITE efforts of some researchers (notably generative linguists) to isolate speech and language function by describing the mechanism of language without attending to the environment, this author feels that environmental influences do alter the output of language. This is not to say that environmental "deprivation" necessarily leads to language "deprivation." On the contrary, the child who develops language skills comparable to those skills commonly used within his environment has developed *functional* and *adequate* language for *that* environment. Rules for language behavior change from culture to culture and the child functions only within his cultural frame of reference. This aspect will be more fully discussed in the following chapter. The present chapter will attempt to identify those sensory-visual-motor skills that are reinforced by environmental experiences and that are prerequisites to language within any culture.

SENSORIMOTOR LEVEL

Piaget describes the first level of awareness and cognitive function as the sensorimotor level (Furth, 1969). The infant's behavior during this period (the first 18 months) is an attempt to structure his immediate spatial surroundings. He develops a spatial awareness of himself in relation to other people and objects. Furth also states that the child perceives only those objects that are personally meaningful and then it is not so much the object that he perceives, but its meaning. This view is supported by Church (1961). The rattle is not viewed as an object (plastic, round with handle, etc.) but as a source of tactile and auditory pleasure. The infant's perception of the world does not involve specifics or details but a perception of the whole or *syncretism.*

Berry (1969) defines syncretism as the comprehension of meaning in the total context. The rattle is comprehended as pleasurable as opposed to painful. There is no reason not to believe that perception of verbal occurrences are differentiated from perception of other occurrences. "Developmentally a sentence does not appear more arbitrary to the two-year old than a thousand other facts, such as the fact that he is not allowed to jump on the sofa" (Furth, 1969). The child eventually uses verbal behavior to verify his perceptual behavior, but in the initial stages of awareness, objects, people and sound are one. He learns to perceive language in much the same way as he learns to perceive objects. "The symbols of speech are one with his gestures, his facial expression, his total action" (Berry, 1969). He cannot analyze individual occurrences or individual utter-

Recognizing the plurality concept of "more or less" begins with minor experimentations. (Courtesy Wood Photographs)

ances. Syncretic behavior controls his awareness of the environment.

In addition to this syncretic behavior, the child is egocentric. Egocentric does not imply selfishness but a limited awareness of self (Piaget, 1969). The child cannot differentiate those experiences that are internally oriented from those that are externally controlled. He becomes totally immersed in his activity so that "when the child is active, his self-awareness is overwhelmed by his awareness of the object he is dealing with" (Church, 1961). He becomes totally involved in the perceptual coding of an object. The rattle is pleasure and he is pleased, are one and the same. He can arrange to some degree, objects according to their perceptual similarities and differences. In the very young child, this arrangement is verified tactually. Taste-testing is one method. Bruner (1969) defines this as the reach-grasp-retrieve-mouth cycle. As the child matures, his perceptions are eventually verified verbally rather than tactually.

PERCEPTUAL CODING

Perceptual coding is eventually limited by verbal coding: " . . . language is even an impediment to perception, obscuring an otherwise direct contact with things as they really are" (Church, 1961). For example, events occur on a continuum while language used to describe these events are constructs developed on linear limits. As Sinclair states (Furth's translation, 1969), "concrete-operational children used operator-like words such as 'more' or 'less' to describe a difference between two continuous quantities whereas preoperational children preferred the use of positives like 'a lot and a little' " The two-year-old can correctly discriminate the relative number of objects in two rows but the three-year-old indicates a longer row with fewer numbers to have "more" (Behler and Bluer, 1969). Although the two-year-old can correctly count a number of things by rote memory, his ability to judge quantity on a cognitive basis is faulty. As he approaches three, he is cognitively aware of quantitive differences but is unable to use one-to-one relationships to consistently establish those differences. In enumeration, the child recognizes that there is more than one (one, two, three, a lot) but he does not realize relativity of counting and summation. This inability to discriminate correctly can be defined as an overdependence on perceptual strategies. Eventually (at 4 ½ years) these children develop a sophisticated integration of conceptual and perceptual strategies. They learn to count the number of objects in each row, ignoring perceptual information regarding length and allowing the conceptual classification of "more" to be appropriately used. In this instance, the conceptual category limited full use of perceptual information.

The child never loses the ability to perceptually code events, but the nature of his particular language determines how much of this perceptual coding will be involved in his verbal constructs.

Perception and Environment

The immediate family environment not only provides food, shelter, and security from the chaos of the world, but it helps to shape the child's use of perceptual information. McCarthy (1954) hypothesizes that "only" children are "afforded greater association with adults, broader experiences and greater opportunities for practice in the use of language." A child with siblings is often more affected by peer group behavior than only children, but ultimately, all children are to some degree influenced by family patterns. Perceptual information is eventually coded along lines set by the environment. Williams and Edwards (1969) studied color concept behavior of preschool children. They found that color and racial concept attitudes were negatively associated with the color black and positively associated with the color white in five-year-olds. In other words, the use of perceptual information was altered by the linguistic codes of the environments of the Caucasian children. Most researchers agree that children associate color to meaning. The concept of color is imbedded in objects and does not exist as an abstract distinction. Color concept formation is thought to stablize later than form concrete formation. Also, since color is not predictable on the basis of a one-to-one relationship with events and objects, it is more susceptible to attitudinal sets.

Linguistic coding of perceptual information does not begin

Language output increases as the need to share ideas increases. (Courtesy Wood Photographs)

immediately. During the early portion of the sensorimotor period, the infant simply does not have enough language to rely on linguistic coding. This does not mean that he is without information. The child who is aware of friction between his parents may be limited by the lack of verbal constructs "fight" or "trouble." He may react to the situation as if the verbal constructs were present when what he in fact perceives is not indicated by the limits of either of these constructs but by his perceptual coding of behavior. Children consistently react effectively to events that they are unable to identify verbally.

The child's ability to perceptually code events in the preverbal period influences the child's behavior later in life. Attitudinal sets begin during this period but are not verbally oriented until much later. "Actions that took place long before the 'rational' mind could be active were found to shape the manifestation of so-called intelligent adult behavior" (Furth, 1969). Without becoming overly involved in the Freudian concept of personality development, those events that take place in early childhood do persist in influencing later experiences. Certainly the value system of the culture is preserved in childhood events, some of which occur in the preverbal stages of development. The youngster *perceives* the relationship of his family to authority figures long before he is *told* how to relate to those figures.

The child's perceptual coding ability is determined by the number of exepriences to which he is exposed. The child who is exposed to a number of events in which he is able to manipulate a variety of items or objects becomes more efficient in prelinguistic skills. "This means that if you have two babies born with equal natural gifts and leave one to lie in his crib for hundreds of hours staring at a blank ceiling while the other is engaged in all sorts of interesting, enjoyable and intellectually stimulating play, the second baby will build an advantage. . . ." (Gordon, 1970). This does not mean to imply that the child learns prelinguistic skills best through materialistic or commerical "games." It does imply that the environment should provide those experiences that will aid the development of spatial awareness, visual perception, and motor coordination. This can be provided by commercial items such as a *Cradle Gym*® or a single plastic ring or spool tied to a string above the baby's bed. Through comprehension and extension. the child begins to structure the world according to his experiences.

COMPREHENSION AND EXTENSION

Furth (1969) defines *comprehension* and *extension* as the general and specific properties of a group of items and the number of items within that definition. First the child perceptualizes the characteristics of an object (comprehension); then, he extends or enlarges the classification by including other items with those characteristics. If the environment never aids him in verifying his perceptions (comprehension), he is less likely to extend the classification.

True, comprehension and extension do not involve significant perceptions until after the child has begun to explore his environment. The initial spatial orientations, however, begin during the sensorimotor period. Below the age of two, visual perception such as distinguishing colors reliably, does not occur. Awareness of body image begins during these initial stages. For example, Church (1961) describes a particular phenomenon occurring during the first year as the "cyclops effect." "Althought he knows at one level that he has two eyes, he experiences them functionally as one; when he tries to peer through a cardboard tube, he plants it squarely between his eyes and is helpless to do anything about his inability to see through."

The one-year-old becomes aware, to some extent, of his own limitations prior to awareness of the limitations of objects. He studies his reflection in a mirrored surface at six months, but it is not until ten months that he begins to show clearcut recognition of his image. At eighteen months, he can recognize a photograph of himself (Furth, 1969). Until well past the eighteenth month period, the child fits round pegs into square holes. His earliest attempts at comprehension and extension are limited by syncretism and egocentrism.

Exploration

Once the youngster reaches the exploratory stage or the stage of ambulation, he appears to be unable to resist testing the environment. This "exploratory drive" dominates his waking moments. The more he sees, the more fascinated he becomes by what he sees. "There are forms that ask to be grasped, textures that invite palpation, and holes and crevices that invite probing with a finger" (Church, 1961). His perceptions often deceive him into believing what is real is not real. Objects change when they are moved, distance changes when something is added, and color changes under different lighting.

Realism, Phenomenalism and Dynamism

Eventually, through this exploratory method, the child learns to categorize things and actions through their properties, characteristics and situational clues. He obtains this information through what Church (1961) calls *realism, phenomenalism,* and *dynamism.* The term realism implies that the child lives in a world that is a mixture of fact and fantasy. All things are possible and he is open to suggestion. "Initially all things are equally real and real in the same sense and on the same plane. . . . " (Church, 1961). This realism is clearly observed in role playing experiences. The youngster who willingly accepts an empty paper towel roll as a horn is exhibiting realistic behavior. It is, perhaps, not practical or logical in the adult sense but to the child it is as equally realistic as the "real" horn.

Phenomenalism is akin to realism. Piaget (1962) theorizes that phenomenalism is accepting causal linkage without explanation. Church (1961) states that for the child "when two events coincide, there is an all but irresistible tendency to experience them as causally connected": "When it gets dark the stars turn on" or "Trees make the wind blow." This type of S-R (stimulus-response) explanation survives "childhood" logic in that some researchers are still prone to explain "unknown" phenomena on the basis of a direct, observable cause-effect or stimulus-response relationship. This does not imply that there are *no* S-R phenomena but in the child's world, phenomenalism is the major explanation of events.

Dynamism is a term used to explain the absence of curiosity about causal connections. The child is willing to accept the obvious explanation as firsthand information. "How did I get here"—"The stork brought you" is not necessarily followed by "How did the stork get here?" In addition, he seems prone to attach significance to miscellaneous bits of information. He then "pieces" together the explanation of events and accepts this explanation as fact. Unanswerable questions are thereby answered and fact is mixed with myth. A child who understands that marriage somehow involves two people who like each other will often insist that she will marry her brother or father. After all, she cannot think of anyone she likes better.

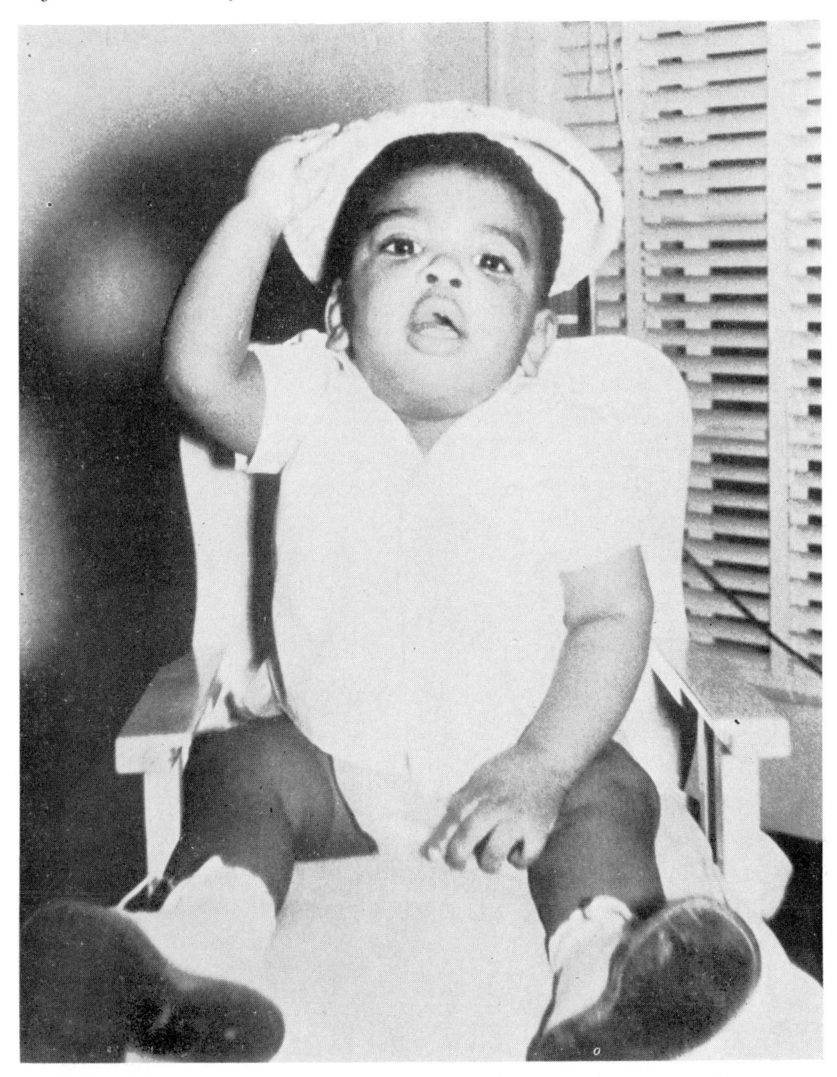

Role-playing may begin with a simple modification of a toy or object.

TEMPORAL REFERENCE

As the child develops a more extended spatial and temporal framework, he relies less on realism, phenomenalism, and dynamism for explanation of events. As he begins to differentiate self from the environment and recognizes events under varied viewing conditions, fact and fantasy separate. Cromer (1968) states that temporal references begin to stabilize at four to four-one-half years. The child at this point is freed from immediate situations and the actual order of events. He begins to hypothesize about the future. His findings are supported by Ervin-Tripp (1970) who stated that "when" was generally the latest form of question for the children in her research to recognize. As late as four years, two months, the children used in this study still found it somewhat difficult to respond to "when did . . .?"

Piaget (1957) also describes this space-time causality organization in which the child recognizes the similarities of events in imagined "displacement." Elkind (1961) also addresses himself to this phenomena by stating that a correct judgment on the part of the child requires that he overcome illusion or distinguish between a real event and its apparent variation. The most frequently used example of this phenomena is the illustration using two balls of clay. The child is presented the clay in the shape of a ball. Then, one ball is rolled into a sausage and the child is asked if they are still the same. The child who is able to visualize the original shape of the clay has developed the ability to visualize events in time-space-temporal relationships.

Church (1961) says that below the age of two, visual form perception seems poorly developed. The six-month-old cannot see that he can obtain a distant, desired object by pulling on the string that lies within easy reach. Colors are recognized as a part of the object rather than independently. Space in back of the youngster is less well articulated than the dimensions of up and down. Two-dimensional patterns (sunlight on the floor) are not defined. "The young child can adapt his grasp to the form of things but is unable to match forms on a form board" (Church, 1961). The world is filled with visual cues that do not exist unless he is actively involved with them.

As comprehension and extension abilities develop more fully, the child is able to incorporate time sequences into practical actions. There is no reason not to believe that language is not governed by a similar sequence. Experiences are first sorted on the basis of obvious similarities. Things that look alike are one and things that sound alike are one. Eventually, his visual and auditory discrimination abilities become more proficient. Sequential ordering of auditory stimuli involves the grasp of time sequences. "They learn language in the same way in which they adapt to customs and regulations . . . rules for walking across the street, rules for games" (Furth, 1969). This learning is sequential just as the ability to differentiate between TOP and POT involves attending to sequential information. The ability to develop the skill is innate or species-specific, but gaining proficiency in the skill is learned.

ROLE PLAYING

This is not to say that learning is the exact structuring of events by the environment. Much of learning takes place through role playing. Role playing is symbolic in that it uses external

Early outbursts of emotion may be the result of frustrations caused by limited mobility.

things and imitative gestures as symbolic representations to service the child's "structures of knowing" (Furth, 1969). The adult's world of ceremonies, rituals, and relationships is symbolized through play. The child can learn to cope with those events that he finds "simultaneously alien, baffling and attractive" (Church, 1969). He also uses play to verify previous experiences. Dusting furniture, playing soldier, playing the "naughty" child and the irate mother, are all symbolic representations that will aid the structuring of future events as well as verify past experiences. The child becomes proficient in gross motor activities (such as arm movements while pretending to sweep) and fine motor coordination (such as imitating the noise of an airplane or "talking" on the telephone). He also develops an awareness of the role of "self" in relationship to the environment.

As a part of the development of "self," role playing allows the child to experiment without the risk of the real situation. It provides him with a method of handling his emotions and frustrations. "The personal habits, inhibitions and items of independence which are specified on the developmental schedule have significance therefore in estimating the maturity of personality. Many of the emotional states like those of fear, anger and jealousy have similiar significance . . ." (Gesell, 1925). Anger is perhaps most often cited since there are so many anger-provoking stimuli in the child's environment. Just sitting on the toilet chair when there are so many things to explore can provoke anger. Being left alone in a room or having his face washed may seem completely "illogical" and frustrating. Anger often leads to fear or vice versa. Church (1961) has stated that the infant's fear of strangers develops only after he has had the chance to come to know his own family. Often the child's fears are based on unfamiliarity and unexpectedness as if to say, "Where did this come from and what does it want of me?" Children become angry or fearful for many reasons. Emotions fluctuate as the child's system of perceptual and conceptual classifications fluctuate.

Imaginative or role play aids the child in overcoming these fears and releasing angers. Of course, it also helps him to prolong positive and pleasurable experiences. In role playing he is all powerful. It is a magic that enables him to establish some degree of control over reality and to influence people and objects. The child's initial play activities are directed toward "self." Although he eventually includes the company of others, his play activity is still directed toward the establishment of identity. Young children spend a great deal of time during play activity giving directions about "who is going to do what, when and how" in order to ascertain their own role in the group. Group behavior is established only when the child has a clear-cut idea of "self."

One of the most important functions of role playing is that the figural correspondent of the original is used to further develop comprehension and extension. This in turn leads to space-time-causality organization. "When a baby assimilates a box to an oral scheme this is due to immaturity, but such is not the case with the doll-playing child who takes the box for a bed" (Furth, 1969). The child finally learns not to be Simple Simon carrying water in a sieve.

CONCEPTUAL CODING

Eventually, the child reaches the stage where he is able to harmoniously work with several components. In other words, he is able to predict several possible ways in which objects might be classified, all of which are, to some degree, evidence of his cognitive abilities (Furth, 1969). His shifting of categories is primarily a conceptual shift rather than a perceptual shift. He is able to analyze characteristics of things and to synthesize these characteristics into some orderly fashion in order to reach conclusions. This is an independent function. He uses perceptual information to develop more complex conceptual categories. He can now anticipate results and reclassify or adjust his actions on the basis of that anticipation. He moves from what Bruner (1969) describes as reach-grasp-retrive-mouth to eye-hand-mind stage. He uses concrete events in a more abstract linguistic sense: ". . . from the abundance of the concrete to the austerity of the abstract . . . the unification of experiences, the reduction of complexity to orderly manageable principles" (Church, 1961). These principles involve space-time-causality

TABLE VI

PSYCHOSOCIAL AND VISUO-MOTOR DEVELOPMENTAL PATTERNS IN RELATIONSHIP TO SPEECH AND MOTOR DEVELOPMENT

Age	*Speech Motor*	*Visual/Motor (Eye-hand coordination)*	*Psychosocial*	
4th wk.	generalized behavior crying activity	follows arc 90°	suck reflex refined	
12-20 weeks	cooing mewing crying holds head erect "discovers" foot	follows moving object 180° hands do not cross over midline circuitous approach primitive squeeze	reach-grasp-retrieve-mouth cycle	Sensori-Motor
6-12 months	rolls over sits up crawls babbling echolalia short attention span first word	grasp under control in order: shoulder-arm-wrist finger pincer movement floor level activity builds "train" with blocks	syncretism egocentrism	
15 months	P-O utterance may begin stands walks yes/no questions attends longer	table level activity but while standing	may "miss" mother	
18 months	runs clumsily plays "ball" hands outstretched answers "wh-" questions accepts chair role play	builds tower with blocks	no cooperative peer play uses comprehension and extension	Perceptual
24 months	uses questions through inflections and "wh" word uses negatives adding "no" P-M-O combinations	arranges toys finishes puzzles	perceptions limit verbal plays side-by-side but not cooperatively	
3 yrs.	imitates movement of train jumping counts, recites, tip-toes	arranges blocks horizontally and vertically, refrains from tower but can use more blocks imitates	order oriented cooperative play attitudal sets begin	
4 yrs.	gives figure a name recognizes two or three colors tries stories	complicated block structure vertically and laterally	dynamism phenomalism realism	
5 yrs.	jumping hops, takes sudden turns inventive naming serial counting increased more temporal references	draws recognizable picture three dimensional block figure imitates	begins competitive play eye-hand-mind cycle	Conceptual
6 yrs.	skipping talks of limitations of blocks	two-dimensional block figure writing some reading	cognitive reality testing	

organization. This organization is based on the addition and multiplication of classes. Upward and downward categorization of information is expanded through his use of perceptual information in the development of conceptual units. He begins to see relationships (causality) based on his increased awareness of the time-space aspects of events.

The preceding chart is a summary of the relationship of psychosocial development to other areas of development. It is imperative to remember that each child proceeds at his own pace. In addition, normative data is at best a guage of the average and never an absolute cut-off level.

The child has more to say and he can use sensorimotor information more effectively. At the same time, his use of perceptual information becomes more culturally bound as he becomes more aware of all the rituals, ceremonies, and modes of behavior associated with his particular environment. Our ability to judge the adequacy of his performance depends on our awareness of the rules of behavior set for him by his environment. The next chapter will deal with cultural influences on linguistic and perceptual behavior.

Chapter Seven

DIALECT: CONSIDERATIONS OF DIFFERENCE

ALL language is a mental game and despite the insistence to the contrary, there are no limits to the extent of play as long as the players can communicate. If one presupposes that a child's language system is designed for adult communication, then it is more than likely that the child will fall short of communication goals (thereby losing the game). The child's system is a mixture of fact and fantasy. If one presupposes that all children will use the exact same rules to play the game, then some of those children will fall short of the communication goal (and it will reflect the theorist's lack of familiarity with children). No two children will perform in exactly the same manner although they may follow the same "patterns" of behavior. This is certainly as true for groups of children as well as for individual children. Yet, research in the area of language acquisition and development is inundated with literature regarding the lack of language development in the child who uses something other than the "standard" mode of communication.

Using Comsky's model of language (reviewed in Chapter Three), it is reasonable to assume that if cognition governs thought processes in the formulation of ideas to be transmitted, those ideas are then mapped into the grammatic rules of a specific language. The rules of that specific language are then transformed into surface structures represented by phonological rules or oral speech. So that the process of deep structure for any dialect of a particular language may be similar while the transformations and surface structures are decidedly different. For example: "She is sitting" and "She sitting" have similar deep structures, but different surface structures. It would be difficult, however, to evaluate competence (a deep structure facility) on the basis of surface structure alone if one uses a "standard" model of surface structures.

We are not referring to specific disorders of neurological deficits, such as aphasia, or disorders attributed to hearing loss or cleft palate. The "disorders" discussed here are those designated as language problems caused by environmental deficit (usually specified as poverty or what this author terms as the "I-ain't-got-no-money,– so-I-can't-talk-good-syndrome").

STANDARD, DIALECT AND BILINGUAL

In the case of the child with a distinctly different dialect or language mode, we must assume that there are rules of linguistic behavior that operate (as with the standard mode) to enable the child to internalize ideas and express ideas within his particular cultural setting.

Contrary to some popular research, there is no *one* dialect system. The Appalachian dialect system is distinctly different from the southern white dialect system. The Appalachian system shares a commonality with black dialects in that it is generally treated as one of the "disadvantaged" language systems (Johnson, 1970). Black dialects range from those most near standard English, such as would be found in middle class urban areas, to the Gullah (Geechee) dialect of South Carolina. In between are variations on the general theme, all English. Bilingualism indicates the existence of two separate language systems. When the bilingual attempts to use English and cannot do so without difficulty, he is often referred to as having a "dialect problem."

A dialect then, is a mode of communication—a language—that consists of a particular set of phonological, grammatical, and semantic patterns commonly shared by a particular group of people in a particular culture and region. Standard English shares the same definition except the latter portion is specified, i.e. commonly shared by the elite and/or educated portion of people who are "privileged" to determine the educational, legal, and business procedures for the country. This, then, distinguishes the *advantaged* from the *disadavantaged.*

The advantaged belongs to that group that can feel some sense of personal identity with goals of the educational, legal, and business processes of the country. In other words, the advantaged group does not feel a need to "join" the society since they already have a voice in that society. To some degree they aid in establishing and developing the "machinery" of society. However, the groups traditionally identified as "disadvantaged" are faced with the *problem* of becoming a part of the "machinery" that establishes the educational, legal, and business procedures of the country. They have little if any voice in the establishment of such machinery. This latter group is often described as having a socioeconomic deficit. It is certainly an economic problem but since social structure is determined by cultural identity, it is hardly a social problem in the usual sense. The social portion of the traditional definition merely reflects ethnocentricity and the unacceptability of cultural plurality.

The idea of cultural identity encompasses much more than economic level. A culture can be defined as a group of people adhering to the same aspirations, achievements, environment, rituals, and most importantly, language. Each of these factors differ from culture to culture although there are some changes within cultures. One might say that geographical location determines the boundaries of a culture; however, modern travel and mass communication have made those boundaries more diffuse than ever. Of those cultural factors mentioned above, language and achievements are perhaps more easily discernible from culture to culture. Achievements would include the number of people from a particular race or creed involved in professions such as medicine, science, or law. It would also include creative achievements such as art or music. Any of these areas are, to a degree, technical. Needless to say, the creative achievements are erroneously viewed as more "primitive and natural" than the professional achievements. You need only recognize that technology can be the development of dyes used in painting or fabric design, as well as development of an IBM machine to see the error of such a judgment.

The aspirations of a culture involve the expectations of future achievements. Middle class individuals are concerned with the balance of work and leisure while less fortunate economic groups are concerned with securing income of any sort. In both cases, the aspirations are fixed. The environment of a culture includes not only the immediate physical environment—food, shelter and clothing—but the family and friends. Children who are raised in a commune find it as "natural" as children who are raised in a one parent family. It is usually the decision of the general society that the physical structure and family structure of a group must meet certain requirements. The rituals of a culture involve religion, social and political celebrations and holidays.

With these definitions of cultural factors in mind, it is difficult to determine the "deficiency" of a culture unless you use a rigid, fixed set of quantitative and qualitative rules for language, environment, achievements, aspirations, and rituals. Such has been the case in the use of the term "culturally deprived." The deprivation occurs when individuals do not (by force or choice) adhere to the guidelines of a given cultural "standard." They do not fit the mode. This is determined not by the persons designated as "deprived" but by the general society (those within the cultural mode). It is quite a shock for an individual to find that he has been considered deprived when he felt all along that his only disadvantage was poverty. Nowhere is the shock more strongly felt than in the area of language. Those who advocate language change use the rationale that such a change will bring about a cultural shift.

The presence or absence of a dialect does not entirely determine one's group identity. The shift of identity must also occur in terms of environment, aspirations and rituals. It must include a denial or reduction of former achievement goals. A change in language patterns may appear to represent a change in cultural groups, but this is superficial. Any cultural change involves acceptance by the group as well as individual changes in behavior and thought patterns. However, what research has done is to use language patterns as a way of identifying cultural differences. Language patterns can be used (quite justifiably) as a way of identifying the degree of ethnocentricity of a country. One cannot, however, use language as a sole determiner of cultural acceptance.

Switching Behavior

If we put the child with a basic language difference in another cultural setting, i.e. the schools, he must either switch to that particular language system and/or translate it into his own language system. We have therefore created or encouraged bidialectal and bilingual communication.

"For example, a person may have a public style which is mostly free of specific Negro dialect features and, in addition, and 'in-group' ethnic style in which the same speaker uses Negro dialect features, especially pronunciation and paralinguistic features plus current in-group slang" (Vetter, 1969). Or, as the preacher says in the Broadway musical *Purlie:* "Some of the best acting is done in front of white folks." Certainly this difference is reflected in research studies such as the ones conducted by Wood and Curry (1969) and Houston (1970). The style of language used during the school situation and other authority-threatening situations is more constrained than the language patterns outside of these situations. This change in patterns or "acting"' ability is referred to as *switching behavior.*

Switching behavior may be receptive; that is, the person can comprehend standard patterns but responds in a dialect. Although receptive switching may exist alone, expressive switching behavior is usually what researchers are referring to and what they use to determine the individual's ability to communicate within the standard or mainstream culture. Despite the Bernstein (1970) and Engleman (1970) theories, the very fact that the children they refer to can understand their directions given in the standard indicates switching ability. This receptive switching ability is certainly evidence of cognitive abilities not ordinarily demonstrated by white children who indeed have a great deal of difficulty understanding some dialects in any form. "That the children of disadvantaged environments are able to understand outside researchers, their teachers, their parents, and each other —often four very different kinds of language—indicates that competence goes far beyond spoken performance," (Houston, 1970).

In both of the above mentioned research studies, it was obvious that the language patterns of black children shifted according to the circumstances surrounding the speech situations.

Penfield (1964) defines this switching ability as a neurological mechanism, a conditioned reflex, that works automatically in the brain. That the child's language was constrained during the school speech situation speaks as much for the situation as it does for his need to develop the lexicon of academia. This need to develop a situation-specific lexicon would be true of any person initially exposed to say, computer programming. The child's awareness of authoritative differences says something about his ability to handle different situations, or, as a popular rock-song of the 1970's stated, "Different strokes for different folks."

Bidialectal and bilingual communication has become the concern of everyone; the educator, the psychologist, the sociologist, and the linguist. They all recognize that there is a difference, but they cannot agree on the significance of that difference. The importance of that significance has been amplified in recent years but the question has not been resolved.

One of the major statements emphasized in the Report of the Kerner Commission was that America is divided into two camps —two cultures. What it failed to emphasize was that this division is supported and nurtured by our insistence on one standard form of English. Those who support standard English argue that language must be grammatically correct and must reflect the highest educational standards of the people. Others argue that it must guard against semantic decay (thereby maintaining an "elaborate" system of communication) and promote standard English communication so that individuals may obtain employment.

RESEARCH TRENDS

It is true that there are some researchers who tend to regard all differences as second language while others regard all differences as an indication of organic deficiency. Studies have "run the gamut" from organic deficiency to linguistic reflection of cultural impress. The following chart is a general summary of this area of study. This chart is designed to show the trend of bilingual and bidialectal research, and not to cite all of the information regarding the subject.

TABLE VII
MAJOR RESEARCH TRENDS IN THE STUDY OF BIDIALECTAL AND BILINGUAL BEHAVIORS

	Organic Deficiency	*Cognitive & Language Deficit*	*Descriptive Linguists*	*Acculturate Methods*	*Utilize Difference*	*Toward Multi-Culture*
1970	Jensen 1969		Williams 1969	McDavid 1969	Erickson 1969	Williams 1969
		Plumer 1968	Baratz 1968	Bereiter 1968	Baratz 1969	Labov 1968
					Shuy 1968	
		Engleman 1967	Engleman 1967	Engleman 1967		
		Entwisle	Labov	Daniel & Giles 1966		
1965		Bereiter 1965	Bereiter 1965	Smiley 1965		
		Hess 1965	Stewart 1964	San Su Lin 1964		
		Deutsch 1964				
1960		Bernstein 1958			Cohn 1959	
		Templin 1958				
		Strauss & Schatzman 1955	Whorf 1954			
		McCarthy 1952				
1950						
	Most research during this period was concerned with social stratification and social class struggle rather than language per se					
1930		Bloomfield 1927				
	Gonzales 1922					
1900	Shaler 1880					
	Morton 1839					
	White 1799					

Organismic Inferiority

The general trend of research began with the anthropological studies of two centuries ago, whereas the trend is now toward a more ethnolinguistic approach. The anthropological theory hypothesized that some individuals are structurally inferior and genetically incapable of achieving the same status as others. Skull measurements were taken to "prove" this theory (Morton, 1839). Later, more "scientific" research was conducted, such as measurement of tongue length and thickness (Gonzales, 1922). Organismic inferiority (racism) was not limited to the study of blacks, although they were the focal point of study. It would be encouraging to say that the age of the anthropologist is over, but to the contrary, the approach is still there under another guise. Recently, Jensen (1969) stated that the middle class white population is separated from the working class white and Negro population not by environment factors but by basic biological and genetic factors. The main thrust of his research is that there is a genetic distinction between black and white, regardless of socioeconomic status. This particular study using the genetic hypothesis was "proven" by the results of standardized tests. What Jensen failed to mention was that the tests had been standardized on experiences more common to the middle class white population than to the lower class population. It is similar to asking an experienced skier to pass a swimming test when he cannot swin while totally ignoring his skiing abilities.

Deficiency Theory

The first major departure from the anthropological view considered "literate" and "illiterate" speech (Bloomfield, 1927, 1933). This view was not so different from the anthropological theory of organismic inferiority of earlier years as one might initially suspect. The "literate" theory still maintained that the superior individuals spoke "good" or "literate" language while the inferior individuals spoke "bad" or "illerate" language. This placed the burden of "good" on those who used a language system much like the written literature originating in Europe or had the European "seal of approval." For while Western man would admit that the Chinese gave Western culture firecrackers and a process of paper making, these same men do not as frequently question the fact that the Chinese are seldom referred to as researchers of the social sciences such as language development. The obvious fault of the literate-illerate theory was that it tended to eliminate a great deal of the world.

This theory persisted for some time, while the country underwent prolonged "birth" throes. Class struggle and social stratification were the topics for language researchers of the following years. The illiterate individual was described as deviant in his attempts to adhere to the prescribed code of behavior. This deviancy was said to be evidenced not only by his verbal output, which was characteristically used as a stereotype, but by the dirth of black writers (and needless to say, reflected in the lack of publishers to handle them).

It was during the twenty year period (1929-1949), that the economic and political state of the country took precedence over literary and literate concerns. The depression era was closely followed by the war years. Research was more concerned with labor needs and manpower. Although there were dialect differences, these were experienced by those poor individuals who could not seem to fit into the pattern of living in this country because of the influence of the "old" country. It was expected that they *would* fit eventually, and they were in fact accepted by the mainstream society once they had adapted accordingly. The question was not "what to do about dialect problems" but "how long before these individuals develop those skills acceptable to a new way of life."

That kind of question persisted until the vast tide of immigrants subsided and the "old" country could no longer be used as a rationale for language differences. The immigrants (unlike the Blacks, Chicanos or Indians) were expected to join. The Horatio Alger effect persisted for them. Dialect surveys of the late 1940's and early 1950's reflected a concern with the phonological influences of the "old" country and geographical mappings of phonological variation rather than the semantic or grammatical differences. This dialect atlas approach based on regional boundaries persisted for some time (Davis, 1970; McDavid, 1965). Educational goals were directed toward maintaining "good" (without "old" country influences) grammar. Advertisement for better speech/grammar were common. It is not that these trends are no longer in evidence, but during those years, the primary concern was "improvement" of the masses.

Specific language research developed as an outgrowth of the dialect survey trend. In addition, the home environment was investigated as a possible source of the "problem." This slight shift to environmental investigations indicated that the impact of successful communicators who had "risen from ranks" could no longer be ignored and so the "problem" took on a new facet. Why do some succeed in throwing off the "stain" and others seem to have a tenacious hold on their "questionable" roots? The answer was soon provided by a division of linguistic systems that smelled suspiciously like "literate and illiterate" with a different title.

It was hypothesized that the dialect system was a restricted system and that the standard system was an elaborate system (Bernstein, 1960). This was evidenced by the failure of dialect individuals to relate to interview questions and test information in the same manner as standard users. It is further evidenced by the lack of similarity between the home structure of the lower class and the home structure of the upper class. This trend has persisted and has become a corporate part of the acculturation methods used to teach the lower class individuals to relate to the world in the same manner as the upper classes. The obvious failure of acculturation, of course, is that its aim is toward discovering and destroying any values of class structure except those of the dominant class.

Whorfian Theory

It is important to note that the Sapir-Whorf theory also originated during the period of dialect survey. This theory, simply stated, says that reality is governed by linguistic structure. Whorf (1956) hypothesized that ". . . human brotherhood begins with a change in language boundaries which in turn develops a culture of consciousness." Both men felt that a language system reflected its culture roots. A language system is adequate if it is appropriate and effective for a particular culture. This theory of consciousness was a divergent step from the trend of ethnocentricity (and still is). Refuse the individual his native language, force him to adhere to your set of rules, and you are promoting acculturation and not a multicultural society. The effects of the Whorfian hypothesis was a cloak of folklore in which many researchers marveled over "strange" customs—for example, the many words for "snow" and no words for "nuclear fission" in the Eskimo language. This kind of folklore is still prevalent in studies in which the main concern is over the colorful and picturesque uniqueness of "hip" or "cool" talk of the ghetto.

Descriptive Linguists

Only recently has there been an effort made to describe the linguistic characteristics of dialect languages. The influence of sociology and psychology on language study has made its impact in this respect. The descriptive linguist attempts to describe not only the linguistic parameters of other language systems, but the conditions that produce and promote this type of behavior. The goal is not to cite the deficiency but to describe the difference.

From these theoretical approaches, we have seen a trend toward the utlization of the difference that will enable the dialect individual to cope with the pressures of a standardized society. The ultimate goal is bidialectalism but the burden of proof still, unfortunately, rests with dialect users and not the dominant society. There have been very few researchers who have seemed willing or able to explore the position that the "problem" is a problem of rigidity on the part of the dominant society, and that if it is to be solved, it must be solved there.

Grammar and Dialect

This resolution does not seem forthcoming. Indeed, the effects of earlier literature in the area are still being felt. The not-so-subtle implications of cognitive and language deficit theories are strikingly similar to the organic deficit theories of earlier studies. It is easy to see how more recent research dealing with language deficit could evolve from the presentation of Morton in *Cranial Inferiority* (1839) or Gonzales in *Thick Lips* (1922). The implications in both of these approaches is that every man must somehow meet a prescribed standard of linguistic behavior (as well as social and psychological behavior). If he does not, he lacks the necessary tools that will enable him to perform in the same manner as the ruling class and he is deficient. Proper grammar has been traditionally used as a means of separating the classes and the deficit theory is no exception.

Let us consider the grammar argument for a moment. Grammar is defined by Langacker (1968) as a set of statements saying how a language works. The speaker internalizes all of the rules of a language necessary to make his concepts (morphemes) functional. A language must follow the principles that govern the ways in which words can be arranged together in meaningful groupings. If this does not occur, then the language is not functional or grammatical. If it does occur, we have established a language system or dialect. You will notice that there is nothing in this definition that implies one *fixed* set of rules. Yet "prescriptive grammarians" insist on one pattern of communication. Other patterns exist but only as *substrata* to a "common" standard. This prescriptive approach is exemplified in such statements as ". . . in some localities [dialect] has become fully standardized, and has even been reduced to rules of phonology, grammar, and syntax. . . ." (Pei, 1967). If it has *ever been reduced,* then, using Langacker's definition, the "reduction" resulted in the development of a more comprehensive language system because it was more widely accepted. It was not the disintegration of a dialect. To accept Pei's reduction statement, however, would in effect condone the primitive/civilized dichotomy of language organization. If a language system is functional for more than one individual, it has rules. As long as it is functional, its growth will be commensurate with the needs of those individuals using that system and, to the contrary, it cannot be reduced.

DIALECTAL RULES

The traditional trend in differentiating "standard" grammar from "substandard" is to say that it is nonstandard, that it has *no* grammar. This is decidedly untrue. Cratis Williams (1967) notes past, present, and future tense delineations for many of the mountain dialects: (leap—lope—lope; light—lit—lit; rake—ruck—ruck). Adrian Dove (1968) notes gender and case for the Afro-American vocabulary: Main man is a woman's boyfriend; a man's closest friend—feminine form is main squeeze. Labov (1970), Baratz (1970), Vetter (1969), and Stewart (1970) have outined the differences between Black dialect and standard English based on their research in this area in the following manner:

1. The zero copula (the verb "to be")
   dialect:
      He out
      She over there
   standard:
      He's out
      She's over there
2. The zero possessive (use of possessive morpheme)
   dialect:
      The lady hat
      The man car
   standard:
      The lady's hat
      The man's car
3. Use of the verb "be" as time extension auxiliary
   dialect:
      He be busy
      He busy
   standard:
      He is habitually busy
      He is busy at this particular moment
4. Subject-verb agreement
   dialect:
      I goes
      He do?
   standard:
      I go
      He does?
5. Negation and past morpheme
   dialect:
      He don't know nothing
      He *don't* know *nothing*
   standard:

He doesn't know anything
He never knows anything

6. Pluralization
   dialect:
   The childrens
   The mens
   Five cent
   standard:
   The children
   The men
   Five cents
7. Articles and prepositions
   dialect:
   I want a apple
   Over to his house
   standard:
   I want an apple
   Over at his house

I must emphasize that not not *all* black dialects contain all of these features nor are these features exclusive to black dialects. It is certainly not the purpose of this book to develop yet another stereotype. A dialect may constitute (in the mind of one researcher) a single grammatic variation or (for another researcher) a number of grammatic variations. The speaker, however, may see no essential difference between his linguistic code and the code of "standard." It should be also recognized that the aforementioned researchers were limited by the scope of their research, i.e. geographical region and number of subjects. What they have attempted to provide is information that would clarify the grammatic variation of a language "difference." Since dialects may also constitute a change in phonological or semantic features, these grammatic variations (which may or may not be present) are only a portion of what is considered language "difference."

STANDARDIZATION INFLEXIBILITY

The inflexibility of standardization can be easily recognized in our inability to accept dialect differences. Instead of assigning intellectual deficits to different dialect groups (as Jensen, 1969, has done), it would be more profitable, both educationally and socially, to accept the differences. Any attempt to discredit the prescriptive grammar theory point by point is successful. So why, then, does the argument continue? Lloyd (1969) has stated that we need to reword the traditional instructions so that we do not designate "bad" or "wrong" or "ungrammatical" to those turns of speech that in actuality are socially unacceptable. "Of course, as soon as people in any given group stop treating, say, aint (*he don't*) as socially unacceptable, it automatically becomes 'correct'" (Lloyd, 1968) (italics mine).

The communication "problems" of the children described by Bernstein and Engleman (1966) and Deutsch (1964) reflect this standardization inflexibility on the part of the researchers, not the children. Even Bernstein's "elaborate" rationalization of his restricted and elaborate code theory fails to alter my impression. His terminology does nothing to alter his basic approach, which contends that dialect speakers fail to adhere to a prescribed code of behavior set by some mythical standard bearers. Labov (1970) argues against this point well when he states, "when it comes to describing the actual difference between middle-class and working-class speakers (Bernstein, 1966), we are presented with a proliferation of 'I think,' of the passive, of modal and auxiliaries, of the first-person pronoun, of uncommon words, and so on." Labov's reaction to Bernstein's approach (and rather aptly I might add) is reflected in Macrorie's description of *Engfish*: "In *the Engfish* paragraphs . . . the words almost never speak to each other, and when they do, they say only, 'Blah'" (Macrorie, 1970).

Bernstein's major thesis is that the elaborate code of behavior offers the individual a more complete and more flexible approach to communication. Labov questions the "completeness and flexibility" of elaborate codes. "Isn't it also turgid, redundant, bombastic and empty?" Perhaps this lack of flexibility on the part of researchers can be more sharply clarified by Entwisle's study. Entwisle (1940) found it "particularly interesting" that black children referred to the stimulus word "black" with responses, pertaining to human beings, whereas white children did not. Academically, it could be argued that these black children have "added" another dimension to a concept. More specifically, it can be argued that the researcher entered the situation with preconceived notions of "right"and "wrong" and did not consider the obvious, the racial connotations associated with the word "black." Perhaps she could have increased her list of *significances* by asking them to respond to the word "white"!

PHONOLOGY AND DIALECT

No measure of language development is considered complete without a phonological study. In the area of bidialectal and bilingual development, phonology has received considerable attention. Templin (1957) has conducted the most standardization studies in terms of categorization of articulation behavior. Her study has been utilized to develop many approaches to the "problem" of dialect communication. Deutsch (1964) has conducted research in the discrimination abilities of dialect children. Burks and Guilford (1969), Clark and Richards (1966), and Eisenberg *et al.* (1968) are only a few of the other researchers who have explored the articulation and discrimination abilities of dialect children.

In all of these studies, results were based on "correct" responses and not appropriateness of response. Appropriateness implies that the response lies within those rules of phonological behavior characterized by the child's dialect and not by some sort of standard, i.e. white middleclass. If the child responds appropriately, then we can begin to make some judgments about proficiency in the area of articulation for that dialect. We cannot say that the child does not demonstrate articulation and discrimination proficiency because he failed to respond "correctly." We can say, however, that the child demonstrates a proficiency that is different from the standard and is based on sound usage of his particular social and geographical environment.

In the case of bilingual children, it is somewhat easier to determine the influences of the "mother" language on English. Spanish children, for example, may show phonological variation in the production of *st* by adding an initial *e,* substituting *ch* for *sh,* distorting *w* and *r* and interchanging *b* and *v*. These variations can be readily traced to the influences of the Spanish language. This "mother" language influence is not so clear-cut for some researchers in the case of dialects. On the other hand, Vetter (1969), Stewart (1965) and Turner (1949) have proposed that the influence of African languages (the mother languages of Black Americans) can be readily traced.

African Influence Hypothesis

The African influence hypothesis is a linguistic approach to the study of bidialectalism. This hypothesis implies that the character of black dialects has been influenced by the Bantu languages, specifically those characteristics involving voice quality, tonal changes, and vowel production. This linguistic background includes such Bantu languages as Bena, Kongo, Suto, and Swahili. Tribes speaking these languages were the main sources of slaves. Thus, the linguistic qualities of those languages are reflected in black dialect.

Gutteral consonants and nasal vowels are more commonly found in Bantu than in English. The variability of such vowel sounds as *eh, ay, oh,* and *aw* may be attributed to the fact that these sounds belong to a single phoneme in the "mother" language, such as Swahili. Therefore, dialect samples may contain "behd" or "bayd" for "bed" or "mehk" or "mayk" for make. In addition, the *b* for *v* may be accounted for by the absence of *v* in some African languages (Vetter, 1969). I feel that what Vetter notes here is the interchangeability of *b* and *v* rather than omission of *b*. Since tonal changes are common in African languages, the wide vocal range of dialect samples is appropriate.

What most researchers count as omission of final sounds, are in fact, assimilation factors rather than omissions. Assimilation occurs when the sound is affected by the preceding or succeeding sound. For example, "what time" in rapid "standard" conversation becomes "wha'time" just as "how are you" often becomes "howaru." An instance of assimilation in dialect conversation is, for example, "righ'on" In other instances, final sounds may be treated in a dialect as an unvoiced stop. In this case the sound is assumed but the movement is not completed. For example, "ea!"/"eat," "swee!"/"sweet," and "tim"/"time." This would be similar to the commonly used standard "bottl"/"bottle" and "tabl"/"table," which are never considered as omissions. In some cases, what traditionally has been considered as phonological deficiences, are, instead, morphological differences. This is exemplified in the previous examples of dialect grammatical variations, "five cent"/"five cents."

Not only are phonological differences evident in segmental phonemes (vowels and consonants), but in suprasegmental phonemes as well. The rate and stress patterns of some dialects show more flexibility than standard English. This often makes it just as difficult for a standard English speaker to comprehend dialect as it does when he attempts to comprehend what he hears on the sound track of a British movie. Stress and juncture in combination with phonological changes are so decidedly different for some dialects that standard English speakers tend to be totally unable to comprehend what they hear(in other words, they are unable to receptively perform switching behavior). Yet it is not uncommon for speakers of dialect to switch from standard stress, juncture, and phonological patterns of the standard to those of the dialect (Wood and Curry, 1969).

Stewart (1970) feels that grammatical variation (cited earlier) as well as phonological variation, may be explained in part through what he calls the "creolization hypothesis." "The nonstandard features of the speech of such persons may be due in part to the influence of the nonstandard dialects of whites with whom they or their ancestors have come in contact, but they also may be due to the survival of creolisms from the older Negro field-hand speech of the plantations."

It is important to attend to all aspects of this hypothesis. It is a plausible explanation; however, it does not account for the identity struggles and oppressions of slavery. Language patterns survive when a culture strives to maintain its autonomy. The influence of the overseer's language patterns does not explain how black dialects have in many respects, patterns that are distinctly different from those standard dialects that were subject to the same influences. Much of what we regard as black dialect was developed as a reaction to the dominant culture rather than contributions from the dominant culture. Stewart's definition should not be taken to mean that dialects developed purely from the influences of several language systems, particularly that of the overseer's.

ATTITUDES AND DIALECT

Students in the area of language development have not only been victims of the researchers' ignorance of ancestoral language influences but also victims of the researchers' preconceived expectancies. Attitudinal sets certainly influence the judgments of the researchers. We have been conditioned to expect a certain type of performance from different social classes. Harms (1961) and Ainsfeld *et. al.* (1962), for example, found listener judgments of standard speakers to be more favorable than judgments of dialect speakers. Researchers often expect the child to behave in a reticent manner, *and* the child views the situation as threatening and somewhat overpowering. Both have been conditioned to the situation and so, act accordingly. Moreover, some researchers make no attempt to alleviate the situation. They walk in asking questions. They seem unwilling or unable to accept obvious answers. If the child responds to "Where is the book?" with a single-word response, it may not indicate failure to use an elaborate code but a cued response to threatening (and sometimes obviously insipid) situation. Many children who are asked a series of limited question by a rather overpowering interviewer will give a series of limited answers. Labov's description of the large friendly white interviewer and the monosyllabic child is a classic example of this situation. (The interviewer's remarks are in parentheses.)

The boy enters the room and is presented with a toy.
(PLUNK)
(Tell me everything you can about this.)
8 seconds of silence
A space ship.
(Hmmmmm.)
13 seconds of silence
Like a je-et.
12 seconds of silence
(What color is it?)
Orange *2 seconds* an' whi-ite *2 seconds*
An' green.
6 seconds of silence

(An' what could you use it for?)
8 second of silence
A je-et.
6 seconds of silence
Give one to some-body.
(Hmm. Who do you think would like to have it?)
*10 seconds of silence
Clarence.
(Hm. Where do you think we could get another one of these?)
At the store.
(Oh ka-ay!)

From "The Logic of Nonstandard English" William Labov, Monograph 22, Report of 20th Annual Round Table Meeting on Languages and Linguistics, Georgetown University Press, Washington, D.C. 1970.

Since Art Linkletter has been making a fortune raising surprising responses from children who speak the "standard," it is no wonder that researchers can *prove* whatever they need to prove by the same method. These same researchers will ask a child who rarely sees a new toy to point out what is wrong with a three-wheeled wagon. In the child's case, it is better than nothing and if you work it right, you can ride it. Or they will ask another child to identify a Christmas wreath when his family barely has enough for one present (if that).

The trend now is to ask about television programs, since children are assumed to do a lot of television watching. More significantly, it is assumed that the child can relate to all of the shows he views. It is rarely imagined that a child will find it rather difficult to empathize with a show that does not portray his way of life or anything closely connected with his personal experiences. Notice, I have said "empathize" which does not directly correlate with the amount of time one spends in any given situation. A black child may find it more relevant to discuss at some length an episode such as the NBC Children's Theatre production of "JT" than many of the "popular" series. In the Children's Theatre production, a ghetto child found it difficult to justify keeping a pet cat when the family could barely manage to support itself. "The Man from Uncle" may be less rewarding for children from an economic area similar to the one depicted on "JT" just as "Gunsmoke" may not be just what the Indian child has in mind as a picture of the "Old West." This is not to imply that dialect language lacks conceptual universals, but it does mean that these children have been culturally alienated from the experiences depicted in some television programs or magazines. These children may find it more difficult to elaborate on the subject if the subject is not relevant. On the other hand, they may elaborate with ease on a relevant subject. As Williams (1970) noted: "Lest the point not be clear, the foolishness of expecting people from markedly different social structures to have common types of abstractions let alone to share them easily in their speech . . . is what I have been trying to illustrate."

ENVIRONMENT AND DIALECT

This insistent pursuit of a standard for language also leads researchers to explore the home environment. McNeill (1966) has been quoted earlier on the hypothesis that the lower class child does not receive the necessary reinforcement for language. This view is shared by others. Olim (1970), Hess and Shipman (1969), and Bernstein (1960) are among those that share this view. Bernstein has divided the family structure into several operational classifications. His conclusion is that the lower class (working family) child is reared in a setting where the family uses directives and their speech lacks abstractions. There is no real evidence to support such a sweeping generalization, particularly since Bernstein conducted most of his studies in England. Yet his hypothesis is widely accepted in this country. Reinforcement differences are not validly clear. "That disadvantaged children are not taught language in the same way as nondisadvantaged, a proposition itself still somewhat in doubt, will not prevent them from acquiring the language of their surroundings" (Houston, 1970).

If Bernstein's description of family structure were to be taken literally, one would expect a grunting, self-centered, loosely run, "live-in." The lack of well-kept lawns may reflect the absence of money for a lawn mower and not apathy over grass. The abundance of rats is not by choice but the result of too many people, without the price of pesticides and without the benefit of public sanitation control, *forced* into unpleasant living conditions. Nowhere in Bernstein's research description is there mention of the outside pressures of social situations. Most often, research refers to the living conditions as if the individuals *desired* such surroundings.

If the family tends to use what these researchers refer to as fewer abstracts (although language itself is an abstraction), it could be that they are reflecting the benefits of that same educational system that is ready to poorly teach the next generation. Perhaps researchers should begin to study the ethnocentric nuances in the language of the teachers of the so-called "disadvantaged" student. Naremore (1971) and Williams (1971) both illustrate how negative attitudes influence student behavior. The increase in directives may reflect the lack of alternatives that could be expected in a lower class setting where strife is more apt to produce imminent danger. The concerns of the lower class family may be more "personal-centered" and less"world-centered" because the lower class family is less close to realizing society's "ambitions" and its comforts. The need to improve the economic conditions of the family overrides the philosophical maneuvers of academia or the theoretical values of one toy over another. It is time that more researchers begin to discuss the cultural deprivers and not perseverate on the deprivees.

Hess and Shipman (1969) are two researchers who hypothesize that behavior which leads to social, educational, and economic poverty is learned. This learning takes place through lack of cognitive meaning in the mother's communication relationships with the child, and a status oriented family structure. The last point implies that the poverty family structure restricts the child's cognitive growth since the child never has the opportunity to become an individual, but is forced through directives to adhere to the code of the group. The child, in other words, is not presented with a number of alternative behaviors, such as in a "person-oriented" structure. Their research attempted to verify these points by interviewing and observing the behavior of 163 black mothers and their children (age four years). Nowhere in their study is there mention of the influence of the dominant society on the lower class family structure. Nowhere in their discussion of interview technique is there mention of tester influence, which Labov has cited as so important.

The status/person differentiation used for lower/upper class (respectively), may imply conditioning to authority dictated by past experiences with the dominant society. Rather than lack of cognitive and conceptual growth, it would seem more pertinent to discuss the ability to learn to survive in a stressful situation. Certainly the survival of lower-class black families has been phenomenal under conditions past and present. It is difficult to believe that the welfare mother would relate to any authority figure in the same way as an upper income mother would. Perhaps what we need is an investigation of the change in cognitive and conceptual behavior of middle-class mothers when placed in an inescapable stressful situation, i.e., the ghetto. As Goodnow (1969) has said, "Anytime we take a task from one culture to another, we must look as closely as possible at what the task demands and what the subject's answer might mean. We may need to change the stimuli or response we ask for, hoping the task will remain the same."

The most glaring aspect of some research is the tendency to regard the lower classes as lacking individuality. "Individuality becomes the privilege of the upper class" (Poussaint, 1970). Conformity is considered a lower class value and any degree of individuality is looked upon as the first step in breaking away from this class structure. This is certainly reflected in the family structure descriptions of researchers such as Bernstein. The status/person or open/closed role system used to describe family units appears to be his way of indicating individuality or the lack of it. It is this kind of division that helps propagate the labels of "them" as if an entire population could be one "voice."

It is important to recognize how the method of research clouds the results. If the family situation is not adequately described, the results of a study dealing with family structure are less than meaningful.

RESEARCH CONSIDERATIONS

What Labov (1969) has stated is true: "When we have discovered how much of middle class style is a matter of fashion and how much actually helps us express ideas clearly, we will have done ourselves a great service." Perhaps Head Start would do well to revise its approach in this regard. Certainly its methods (as simplistic as they might be) are developed on the principle that they are providing this child with some middle class values, and that through these values he will develop the tools that he needs for successful education. What research needs to do is take a look at standarized communication. How much of what a child does with communication is necessary for certain situations and what sorts of situations will be appropriate for this child? How do we get him involved and keep him involved in successful communication rather than attempting to steer him toward some mythical standard?

A comparison of responses for certain situations for both dialect and standard users would be useful only if the standard were asked to respond to situations common to the dialect as well as vice versa. The question is not what style is necessary for communciation but what is appropriate and effective in terms of the speech situation.

DEVELOPMENTAL CONSIDERATIONS

The child's language style changes as he approaches the adult's mode. Some research studies, as previously mentioned, imply that the dialectal and bilingual child fail because he does not operate within the standard adult mode. More significantly, some research studies compare the dialectal and bilingual adult communication patterns with the dialectal and bilingual child's pattern. It is refreshing to note that the descriptive linguists have attempted to make the distinction between the childhood and adult patterns. As Houston (1970) says, "Whereas child language always differs qualitatively as well as quantitatively from adult language, no childhood stage of any language is appreciably simpler or more randomized than the corresponding stage of any other language." In other words, the black child develops language patterns with holophrastic utterances and pivot-open classifications in the same manner as any other child. It is that his environmental (adult) coding model differs so that his eventual language structures, as described by transformational grammars, will have different surface structures but similar base (noun-phrase, verb-phrase) structures.

It is hypothesized that the black child develops a language

system that contains more "downward" classifications because of his restricted environmental situation. Remember that downward classification indicates addition to a category (car—Ford, Chevrolet, etc.) and not the direction of the category. Since the dialect child does not have the commercial playthings that other children may have, this theory would not appear to be true. The dialect child relies more on word games and imagistic role play, perhaps, than children from a standard language background. He sees the three-wheeled wagon is viable because he can imagine the other wheel and a dozen other uses for the wagon, whereas a child from a more stable economic situation immediately notes that the wagon is inoperable because of the missing wheel. "Perhaps because they were quite poor and had little material with which to play, dialect childen engaged in constant language games, verbal contests, and narrative improvisations far removed from linguistic disability" (Houston, 1970). This reordering of language priority is also mentioned by Claude Brown (1968) and Kochman (1969). It is possible that another failure of Head Start lies in their tendency to ignore this as a viable force and use commercial toys as a means of providing a success situation for these children.

Aside from the obvious grammatical differences offered by the adult code of the environment, the aforementioned extension of language function appears to be the greatest difference in the acquisition of language structures. Menyuk (1970) cites examples of linguistic units that are limited to children's grammar only, in what is termed "the low income strata." Her research indicates that these characteristics are similar to patterns found in standard childhood grammars. Cazden (1970) cites the case of Gerald, a thirty-three-month-old black child, whose sentence length is longer than the average sentence length noted for standard childhood utterances. Dialect and standard language youngsters appear to generalize noun and verb endings to the same degree (Shriner and Miner, 1968). This is also true of their ability to respond to questions involving the meaning of nonsense words in sentences (LaCivita, Kean and Yamamoto, 1966). As noted earlier in this book, field workers have found that all children of different cultures acquire language at approximately the same developmental period. It would appear that although language is structurally different from culture to culture, the developmental sequence is the same.

There are some consistent and distinct bilingual differences that are directly attributable to the amount of influence of the mother language. Unlike the dialect child, the bilingual child has a direct conflict of grammatical structures. The dialect child develops adult grammatical structures that are a variation of the adult Standard English grammar structures. The bilingual child develops grammatical structures that are influenced by the amount of "mother language" involvement. The amount of research on bilingual influences is extensive. Werner Leopold (1949) has edited an entire series of volumes on the developmental aspects of bilingualism. Although the variations from standard English may be similar to those variations found in dialect systems, the common misconception that these children may be grouped together when considering language differences is misleading. Their commonality is their exclusion from the mainstream society rather than language coding. The society's intolerance of any language system other than the standard forces these children to share the same "problem." The historical emphasis on one language system is as strongly felt by the Indian child who was physically punished for speaking his native language as the black child who is programmed via Engleman's (1970) rote memory approach (Baby-see-the-cat idea, similar to See-Dick-See-Jane). Physical retaliation for not using the "standard" is still reported. Chicano children have been similarly alienated when they are not allowed to use the linguistic coding system most available to them for self-expression.

Any "deficits" that occur in bilingualism appear to occur not because of developmental lag, but rather because of transfer or translation difficulties. The results of a study conducted at McGill University in Montreal indicated that ten-year-old bilingual children showed greater intelligence than monolingual children of the same age (Penfield, 1964). Indeed, research has yet to show that the sequence of basic structural development of linguistic coding is affected by bilingualism. For example, Riley (1968) investigated word recognition and Anastasi and deJesus

(1953) investigated sentence length and syntax. Both research studies found no basic differences between performances of the English and Spanish speaking children. It should be noted that both studies allowed the children to use the other language systems as they needed them without penalty.

It would appear, however, that the availability of language transfer is often inhibited (John and Horner, 1970). When the child is not allowed to use his "mother" language freely, he experiences transfer difficulties that have been interpreted as true grammatical deficiencies. For example, bound morphemes (plurals and verb tense endings) are greatly affected by transfer availability, so that "jumped"–"jumpted" and "men"–"mens" may appear in Chicano dialects. Responses of this nature would penalize a child on certain test instruments and the results would indicate a language deficit if taken at face value. Phonological influences, such as those mentioned earlier in this chapter, may also characterize language change. Many of these changes are similar to dialect changes and yet the basis for bilingual change is rooted in a language system that is not English in origin.

To make the transfer to English, the child is required to adapt English coding referents as well as English vocabulary. Often this is difficult because there are no Spanish words for equivalents for English referents. For example, Spanish has no single-word equivalent for the English word *cheating*. In addition, the suprasegmental phonemes are transferred from the "mother" language into English. When this occurs, the rate, stress and rhythm patterns of English speaking Chicanos are often more Spanish than English. Our ability to understand bilingualism and bidialectalism depends greatly on our ability to understand the present and historical culture patterns of these groups as well as their present language patterns.

MULTICULTURAL APPROACH

The more we insist on a rigid and monocultural language pattern the more we will promote stereotype and prescriptive research. Until there is more literature that will clearly define the parameters of dialect languages, we cannot hope to develop a language culture of consciousness. Language is the medium of the culture. The ideas of that culture is the message carried by that language. Each culture has its own language system. In a multicultural society, there are many variations of the same language system. "Standard" language is only one of those variations, only one of the many dialects of a multicultural society.

We need to understand the unconscious effortless manipulation of other linguistic systems; manipulations that though different are intricately, manifoldly systematized (in terms of order, harmony and beauty) and intellectually complex (in terms of

Figure 13. Each child expands his language in accordance with the environment and not the prerequisite of a "standard" culture (after Camper).

subtleties and penetrating analyses of reality) (Whorf, 1954). We must understand that all language is a highly structured intellectual game played by long forgotton rules. There are no primitive language systems. If we are to participate in the game, then we must make the effort to learn the rules and not disparage the game simply because it does not use these rules most familiar to us. Since the process of social change is set by the mainstream society, then that society must take it upon itself to "reduce the circumstances which perpetuate and increase ethnocentrism" (Williams, 1970). We cannot hope to explain the manipulations of a dialect child's language structure without some knowledge of that structure.

> "Speak for yourself," said the egg woman.
> "I can't speak for anyone else, I don't know the language."
>
> —CAREY, *The Horse's Mouth*

Chapter Eight

EVALUATION OF LANGUAGE DEVELOPMENT

IT is often very difficult for the beginning student of speech and language development to realize that the overall developmental sequence is involved in the evaluation of language skills. Ellingson (1967) in *The Shadow Children* cites the following prerequisites for language development:

> In the Areas of Visual Perception and Discrimination a child must be able to—
> do directional activities
> understand differences in geometric forms
> have the ability to do sequential geometric form skills
> see and understand likenesses in abstract figures
> know laterally—his right from his left hand
> have visual discrimination for objects
> have visual discrimination for details in pictures
> have the ability to complete pictures
> have visual discrimination for gross symbols
> be able to perform perceptual constancy skills
> discriminate the differences in form and position of objects
> have perception of spatial relationships
> have ability for comparing and contrasting configuration of words
> be able to perform figure-ground perception
> be able to perform visual-motor skills
> discriminate differences in gross symbols
> discriminate differences in horizontal and vertical lines and curves in making words
> know his position of body in space
>
> In the areas of Auditory Perception and Discrimination a child must be able to—
> understand common words as spoken

be able to perform listening skills for differences in words
be able to reproduce (imitate) three syllable words
be able to perform rhythmic training skills
be able to perform digit drills for attention span
have recognition and discrimination of common sounds
be able to reproduce rhyming sounds
be able to recognize words to rhyme with pictures
give initial consonant sounds to pictures
be able to hear initial medial and final sounds in words.
be able to hear vowel differences
be able to hear and reproduce vowels, consonants, and consonant blends
have recognition and discrimination of similar sounds

In the area of Comprehension a child must be able to—
be able to classify common objects
have a concept of when, where, what and who
understand sequence of events
have ability to anticipate holidays, etc.
have a concept of direction words—stop, go, etc.
have a concept of up, down, first, last, etc.
be able to interpret pictures
be able to follow a picture sequence
be able to draw conclusions
be able to match color names to colors
be able to associate action with words, come, run, etc.
have developing knowledge of community workers
understand differences between fact and fantasy
be able to follow one-step directions
be able to classify ideas
have concept of singular and plural

Most of the prerequisites are recognizable as subsections found on various intelligence tests. The evaluation of that elusive human property known as intelligence involves the use of language and language skills. Yet the inherent purpose of intelligence testing is the measurement of innate constitutional properties that are not exclusively language (or language oriented). Since there is so much variation from test to test (each test supposedly designed to measure the same function), Church (1961) proposes that factor analysis may be a technique for finding exactly what one puts into a test in the first place.

INTELLIGENCE TESTS

Intelligence (by this author's definition) is defined as the ability to operate effectively in a symbolic and cognitive sense through the use of sensorimotor information (spatial-temporal-causal relationships); the ability to be independent, flexible, and adaptative in social and interpersonal situations. This definition does not preclude the use of language nor does it imply that language is the sole means of intellectual function. "Progress in logical thinking is in *no* obvious way linked with progress in linguistic ability" (Furth, 1969).

What the intelligence test often tends to measure is the individual's ability to handle the test situation. Menyuk (1970), Labov (1970), and Church (1961), commented on this point. The most significant aspect of their comment is that intelligence tests are geared toward middle class values and the middle class child is equipped with some degree of "test wisdom." His expectancies for the test situation are more positive than those of other children. The test situation and test information are perhaps more familiar and, therefore, more positively reinforcing than for other children.

Culture Free Tests

The cultural biases of intelligence tests have come under close scrutiny in the last fifteen years. Most modern researchers would seem to agree that intelligence tests are unfavorably biased toward the child who cannot anticipate a pleasurable school experience and/or who has not had the opportunity for such an experience. Culture-free tests have been attempted; however, linguistically oriented tests have little hope of ever being entirely culture free. This is based very simply on the intrinsic nature of language. As we have discussed in previous chapters, the child's orientation toward language and his use of perceptual coding is determined by his past experience, i.e. culture and immediate environment. There is no reason to expect that a linguistically oriented test can hope to include all of the linguistic variations of any society.

Cattell (1940) devised a "culture free" test (the IPAT Culture Free Intelligence Test) which was designed to decrease the effects of cultural differences in the measurement of intelligence. The test is nonverbal and untimed. It attempts to avoid items involving spatial perception and manipulative ability which Cattell feels do not effectively measure intelligence. It does attempt to predict verbal achievement without heavily weighing the test with items involving verbal and fluency factors. Although research studies have noted some differences in performance scores for children on the Cattell when compared to such measures as the Binet and Weschler, these differences are not significant (Willard, 1968; Marquart and Bailey, 1955). It would appear, however, that cultural differences influence the results of the Binet and Weschler to a somewhat greater degree than the Cattell. "One cannot be certain, of course, what level of freedom from cultural influences is attained by this scale, but the test results from it seem to be less influenced by economic status than are those obtained from the Stanford-Binet" (Marquart and Bailey, 1955).

Other researchers have demonstrated how cultural bias can influence performance scores by designing instruments that are specifically geared toward certain cultural groups. These tests are primarily utilized to demonstrate how ineffectively some traditional standardized test instruments measure ability outside of the mainstream. One such test is the Dove Counterbalance Test of Intelligence, (Dove, 1968) which is a test of verbal skills. My experiences using this test indicate that Black students respond significantly better than do Caucasian students. The test is not designed to show how well black children can perform on an instrument specifically designed for their culture, but rather to demonstrate the invalidity of instruments standardized on the mainstream culture to measure ability for other cultures. It is doubtful whether a cultural free test can be effectively designed to measure abilities in *all* cultures. Attempts such as the Cattell and the Dove should be used to demonstrate the need to revise the development and standardization of test instruments.

There have been some attempts to develop tests that are specifically designed for bidialectal linguistic abilities. Baratz (1969) has developed a measurement for assessing language on a bidialectal task. This includes stimulation of responses and is basically a repetition task. It does not, however, give us standardized information about dialectal language performance norms systems comparable to existing test instruments concerned with standard language systems.

Test response, like any response, may be hampered by any number of circumstances. These circumstances may be constant or momentary. Certainly, any individual who is suffering from an illness or disease may find it difficult to respond in the same manner as he might when he is well. Intelligence tests consistently fail to account for "social malaise." "For example, the influence of malnutrition and of diseases that delay development is higher among poor children who may also be emotionally less amenable to testing situations than those from carefree homes" (Lenneberg, 1966). Some researchers tend to view this phenomena as one brought on by the sufferer as if the lower class individual masochistically imposes on himself those factors that limit his ability to become a part of the mainstream of society. They are, in effect, accusing minority cultures of injecting themselves with bias by implying that their inability to successfully respond to tests (which have been standardized on middle class individuals) is learned

There are those researchers (as pointed out in the previous chapter) who insist that some responses are more adequate than others. They maintain, therefore, that intelligence tests measure the child's adequacy, and if children from "sub"-cultural backgrounds fail to be successful on such tests, it simply points up the basic weakness of the culture (or the children) (Jensen, 1969).

Test Limitations

"There is no reason to believe that any society has a monopoly on the organic constitutional factors which permit the development of intelligence" (Church, 1961). Indeed, if tests fail to point out how one child is more equipped for performance activity or the ability to fend for himself under a certain set of circumstances, then the test and not the child or culture has the low "IQ." Certainly the black child develops a language code that helps him communicate in his environment. The white child would find it very difficult to cope with the social climate or the language of the ghetto, yet this would not constitute a genetic/intelligence weakness.

Most important in this consideration of test adequacy is the assumption that children will develop the same linguistic context for events regardless of culture. To be sure, children of similar backrounds will obtain similar linguistic connotations. However, there will be some variation even among children of similar linguistic and cultural backgrounds. Since most tests allow for limited "right" or "correct" responses, these variations are not taken into account.

A few of the limitations of contextual significance to linguistic codes have been noted by Church (1961) and are as follows:

1. Vocabulary tests: definitions hint of the egocentric, concrete action-bound way in which children apprehend reality and of their own experiences to others.
2. Concept-formation tests: the ability to specify either differences or similarities comes later than the ability to react to them.
3. Object classification tests: earliest approaches to sorting realistic objects are contextual; the objects belong together because they occur together in real-life situations.

Most tests assess the quality of existing language development but not whether children are actually not capable of taking advantage of existing stimulation (Lenneberg, 1966). The importance of recognizing the limitations of test instruments is not the elimination of the instrument, but an awareness that brings about caution in the interpretation of results. Given a large enough sample and a comprehensive knowledge of statistics, a researcher can "prove" almost any theory. The conclusions of the examiner alter the effectiveness of any test. If the examiner has a tendency to generalize to a population beyond the frame of reference of the test and population used to validate the test (or beyond his frame of reference for that matter), then the test has not served the purpose for which it was designed.

TYPES OF TESTS

Test instruments designed specifically for very young children are often called developmental scales. These tests usually involve some sort of checklist of observable behavior; that is, the examiner is required to note specific skills based on normative maturational data from previous research. Other test instruments call for manipulation of concrete materials and the completion of items require more active participation of the child. The third type of test is one in which the child is required to make some sort of verbal response. There are various combinations of these three basic forms. Some are sub-test variations of the first two basic types. Others are verbal-nonverbal variations of the second two basic types. Still another variation will involve only verbal responses with a minimum inclusion of the other types.

The primary purpose of any test instrument should be the measurement of a child's abilities. The test should measure what he *can* do in a specific area of development rather than point out his primary deficiences. If a test repeatedly eliminates a particular group of children, then the test should be reexamined and revised. Several tests have been specifically revised for neurologically impaired and/or motor handicapped children. These tests will not be reviewed here. It is our purpose to include only a sample of test instruments that to some degree measure those prerequisites for language listed at the beginning of the chapter. It is to be understood that *any* test may be used to investigate development disorders as long as the child is not subject to a priori penalities of standardization procedures. A comprehensive look at the evaluation of the linguistically handicapped child can be found in such volumes as *Language Disorders in Children* (Berry, 1969 and *Psychological Testing* (Anastasi, 1961).

Test Samples: Intelligence

Two of the most widely used intelligence tests are the Stanford-Binet and Weschler Scales. The Stanford-Binet was one of the first standardized measures of intelligence. It was originally developed in France in 1904 as the fruit of Binet's earlier research (Anastasi, 1961). Binet used the first scale (the Binet-Simon Scale) in an effort to determine the number of retarded children among the low income groups of that country. It was adapted for use in this country by the Stanford Universtiy research team in the early 1900's. In 1916, Terman standardized the first revised American version on California school children. At least one-third of the original items were retained. In 1937, the Stanford-Binet was again revised and the scale increased on a standardization population of 3,184 Caucasian children. Since then, there have been two additional standardization revisions and regroupings of the basic forms called L and M (Anastasi, 1961). The items have remained essentially unchanged from the 1937 version. Standardization groups, although larger, are similar to earlier groups and are not a representative sample of American school children. What we are using in the Stanford-Binet in 1971 is similar, although not identical, to the items used to test retarded children in France nearly a century ago. In addition, although the test is used for cross-cultural study, the norms have not been changed significantly in over a decade.

The Stanford-Binet contains standardization scores for ages 2.6 to 8 years. This test is highly structured and requires many verbal responses. The child is restricted to a limited number of "incorrect" responses and must be able to comprehend verbal instructions before attempting any of the subtests. Stimuli used in the test instrument presumes past experiences with similar information. It also contains timed subtests. Since the penalty rate is high for nonverbal, language-different and uncooperative children, this test should never be used as the sole measure of ability if the tester has any questions regarding the validity of his results. The test is often used as a measure of a child's ability to attend to information most often found in middle class settings and as such, is said to be a predictive means of determining a child's performance under those conditions. These results should not be interpreted, however, as innate ability.

The Weschler Scales (Weschler, 1949, 1963) are divided into three sections: The Weschler Adult Intelligence Scale (WAIS), the Weschler Scale of Intelligence for Children (WISC) and the Weschler Preschool and Primary Scale of Intelligence (WPPSI). We will attend to the last two scales. Neither of these scales contains cross-cultural standardization. The second scale (WISC) contains standardization scores for ages five to fifteen years. The WISC contains twelve subtests designed to measure verbal and performance responses. It is questionable whether this particular type of learned information can be used as a measure of innate intelligence. It can, however, be used as a measure of retention of information gained during highly structured educational training; for example Who wrote "Paradise Lost"? Why is flour used in making bread? Define mausoleum.

The WPPSI contains standardization scores for ages four to six years with more cross-cultural validation than the WISC. Again, the subtests are divided into verbal and performance areas. The test is designed with the assumption that the young child is primarily sensorimotor directed and that although he is capable of using appropriate language structure, he may have difficulty specifying either the differences or the similarities of his choice. The verbal subtests can be effectively used to determine a child's ability to function with verbal information more pertinent to traditional classroom settings; for example, What is the thing to do if you are sent to buy a cake and the store owner says he does not have any more?

2 points: Borrow some from a friend
0 points: Make some.

It is obvious that in a rural area, a child may be more prone to answer "make some," whereas in a communal setting a child might answer "borrow some." One wonders how the child of a metropolis the size of New York (infamous for its "don't get involved" attitudes) might respond. In all three cases, the child will offer the "right" answer, right in that it is appropriate to his past experiences. Yet the child's right answer may lead a tester to doubt his innate capabilities if the test is taken a point-by-point face value. The WPPSI does, however, contain more of the performance items noted at the beginning of this chapter than the two previously mentioned test instruments. As such, it is a more adequate measure of the development of those language prerequisites.

The Leiter International Performance Scale contains items that are designed to measure performance from year two to eighteen (Leiter, 1950). The child is required to demonstrate organization of visual perceptual information. The use of this type of informantion is prerequisite to cognitive-linguistic function. He must demonstrate his ability to adapt to the environment by inserting picture blocks in the appropriate slots of a frame containing a stimulus card of matching pictures. The items involve categorization (such as hat-to-head, shoe-to-foot), matching colors and forms, analogies, picture and series completion, spatial relationships, and numerosity. The items represent a wide range of function and are as diversified as those found on verbal tests. The test has no time limit. Verbal instructions are to be kept to a minimum and in some cases, such as with a deaf child, can be replaced by gestures. Since verbal performance and instructions are not an essential part of the test, it can be effectively used with bilingual and bidialectal children. The Leiter has been standardized on a wider cross-cultural sample than most other tests. Standardization populations include Chinese and Japanese children, Mexican children, middle class white American children, and children from the Bushman tribes of the Kalahari and Ngamiland regions of South Africa. Because the test utilizes blocks and bright colors, it can be effectively administered to young children without losing their attention. It is one of the few existing test instruments that can be used with a wide variety of children who may be at a disadvantage with a verbal test of the Binet type (Orgel and Dreyer, 1955).

Test Samples: Visual/Motor

The Raven's Coloured Progressive Matrices was thought to be one of the first truly culture-free tests (Raven, 1960). It was developed in Great Britain. The Raven's involves visual organization or what is called by some researchers, Level I-cognitive ability. There is no time limit and minimum verbal instructions are required. The child is required to find the missing portion of the designs or matrices from a selection of six or eight choices. There are three sets of Coloured Progressive Matrices. Each set contains problems of increasing difficulty involving serial completion, parts-to-whole and analogous designs. Results compare the child's performance with other children of that age (using percentiles) rather than a computed IQ or age norm. Although the Raven's still holds promise as a cross-cultural index of cognitive function, results of studies have not been valid or consistent enough to warrant more than speculation regarding the full scope of its use.

The Oseretsky Motor Development Scale contains standardization scores for ages four to fourteen years. It was originally designed by a Russian researcher and has since been standardized in this country. The latter two versions (the Vineland-Oseretsky and the Lincoln-Oseretsky) have both been widely used. The older of the two, (Vineland-Oseretsky) contains sixty of the original eighty-five items, six for each age level (Doll, 1946). It is the most difficult to administer and has been used less often than the Lincoln-Oseretsky. The Lincoln version

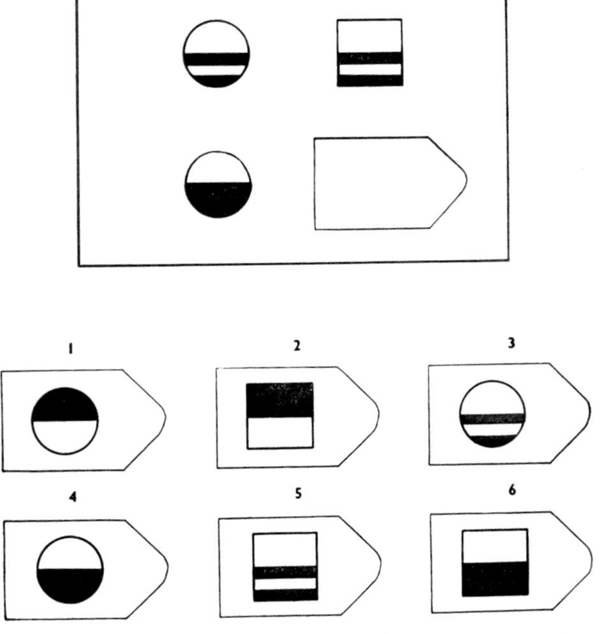

Figure 14. Plate B-8 from Raven's Coloured Progressive Matrices, by J. C. Raven © 1960. (By permission of H. K. Lewis, London.)

is less difficult to administer and contains only thirty-six items (Sloan, 1955). It has also been more specifically designed to allow for cross-cultural testing. They both involve items of locomotion (walking, hopping, etc.), gross motor control (catching a ball), and fine motor coordination (pencil and paper tasks).

Test Samples: Preschool

The Communicative Evaluation Chart is a checklist of overall maturation including items from the Gesell, Binet, Cattell developmental scales (Anderson *et al.*, 1963). Items begin at the three-month level and continue to the end of the fifth year. It demands little structure and can be used with children who have difficulty performing in standardized test situations. The results do not yield an age score or IQ, but can be used as a quick appraisal of level of general performance or language ability up to age five. The nonverbal items are in the right hand column (see Fig. 15) while the verbal items are in the left hand column. The child is allowed to proceed at his own pace and an estimate of his verbal and nonverbal performance levels would be indicated by the highest year containing correct responses. As in the case with many maturation guides, it is an adequate method of subjectively evaluating a variety of children.

The Receptive-Expressive Emergent Language Scale (REEL) is the newest preschool scale available (Bzoch and League, 1971). Although it is very lengthy (132 items on an eight-page recording form), it does attempt to evaluate both the encoding (expressive) and decoding (receptive) aspects of language potential. Despite its length, the estimated time of administration is ten minutes. A combined language age score (CLA) can be computed by adding the expressive and receptive language response. The scale can be used for children up to the age of three. The responses are measured through observation and parent interview. Since the scale has had limited use, its applicability to cross-cultural populations is still in question. It is important to note, however, that standardization procedures were conducted on fifty infants from"enriched linguistic environments." In addition, the standard grammatic code is often used as a means of judging the correctness of expressive responses. Because it attends to prelanguage and early language skills, it is likely to be a useful instrument in that area. Its value, however, lies in the distinction of receptive and expressive responses.

The Merrill-Palmer Preschool Scale (Stutsman, 1931) and the Minnesota Preschool Scale (Goodenough *et al.*, 1932-1940) are two of the most popular preschool test instruments. Both contain verbal and nonverbal performance items. The Merrill-Palmer contains fewer verbal items and as such does not yield comparative information about these two areas. The Minnesota is more of a balance of verbal and nonverbal tasks.

The Merrill-Palmer involves items of language expressions such as "What is this?" and "What runs?" The performance tasks require many coordinated responses (such as cutting with scissors and paper folding) as well as visual-motor responses (puzzle completion and matching colors). The Merrill-Palmer is suitable for ages twenty-four to thirty-six months. Standardization of the Merrill-Palmer does not include cross-cultural populations. In addition, the child is penalized by items requiring speed as well as skill. It is a relatively easy test to administer in that each item (concealed in a brightly colored box) is designed to hold the child's interest and curiosity.

The Minnesota contains verbal items of comprehension as well as expression. Although its verbal items are more extensive than those of the Merrill-Palmer, there are some weaknesses. For example, the pictures to elicit verbal expression responses ("Tell me all you can about this") are of the early 1900's genre both in the clothing of the people depicted and in the outmoded occupation of one of the pictures. Many children would find it difficult to discern the activity in the 'tintype" photo in addition to their lack of familiarity with that type of activity. Other verbal items include pointing to objects or body parts of a doll, naming objects from memory and vocabulary items as opposites. Performance items span a degree of complexity from form discrimination, tracing forms and puzzle completion to paper folding and imitating the hands of a clock. The Minnesota is designed for ages eighteen months to six years. The Minnesota also has not been standardized on a cross-cultural population. In addition,

COMMUNICATIVE EVALUATION CHART

NAME ____________ SEX ________ DATE ________

BIRTHDATE ________ AGE ________ EVALUATOR ________

LANGUAGE LEVEL ________ PERFORMANCE LEVEL ________

1 YEAR

Good chewing, sucking and swallowing movements ____ ____
Understands gestures ____ ____
Listens with understanding to words ____ ____
Obeys command: "Give it to me" ____ ____
Imitates a variety of sounds ____ ____
Knows Mama and says "Mama" ____ ____
Knows Daddy and says "Dada" ____ ____
Attempts new words ____ ____

Stands without support ____ ____
Plays games with more understanding ____ ____
Is developing a sense of humor ____ ____
Opens a small box ____ ____
Marks with a pencil ____ ____
Inserts spoon in a cup ____ ____
Alerts visually to many new things ____ ____
Interested in playing with people ____ ____
Repeats performance when someone laughs ____ ____

1½ YEARS

Good movements of tongue, lips & palate ____ ____
Understands simple questions ____ ____
Identifies objects by pointing ____ ____
Points to own nose, eye, mouth, hair ____ ____
Extensive vocalization and echoing ____ ____
Has speaking vocabulary 5-10 words ____ ____
Uses 2 word phrases; short sentences ____ ____

Walks unassisted ____ ____
Catches and throws ball crudely ____ ____
Shows preference for certain toys ____ ____
Beginning to feed self with a spoon ____ ____
Places □ and ○ in formboard ____ ____
Imitates a 2 to 3 block tower ____ ____
Makes marks with a pencil ____ ____

2 YEARS

Eats table foods including chewy meat ____ ____
Responds to: "Show me a dog" ____ ____
Responds to: "Show me a man" ____ ____
Responds to: "Show me a hat" ____ ____
Can point to doll's eye, nose, mouth, hair, hand, foot, etc. ____ ____
Follows simple directions ____ ____
Names familiar objects: ball, dolly, etc. ____ ____
Has discarded jargon ____ ____
Says simple phrases and sentences ____ ____
Uses nouns, verbs & some pronouns ____ ____
Answers: "What is your name?" ____ ____
Answers: "What does the doggy say?" ____ ____
Answers: "What does the kitty say?" ____ ____
Has approximately 300 word vocabulary ____ ____
Has 25% use of consonants ____ ____

Turns pages of a book singly ____ ____
Spontaneous scribble with a pencil ____ ____
Imitates circular motion with pencil ____ ____
Makes a tower of 3 or 4 blocks ____ ____
Puts together a 3 piece peg toy

____

Completes 3 piece formboard forward ____ ____
Beginning to match 2 like objects or simple pictures ____ ____
Plays meaningfully with toy dolls and toy furniture ____ ____
Kicks large ball ____ ____
Walks; runs fairly well ____ ____

FIRST PRINTING . . . MARCH, 1963; SECOND PRINTING, REVISED EDITION . . . SEPTEMBER, 1964
PUBLISHED BY EDUCATORS PUBLISHING SERVICE, INC. 75 MOULTON ST., CAMBRIDGE, MASS. 02138

Figure 15

there are so many items that it is sometimes difficult to keep the child's attention througout the test. Since attention factor is very important in any consideration of the preschool population, this is not advantageous.

Test Samples: Social/Language

The Vineland Social Maturity Scale is a widely used assessment of social maturity that involves interviewing the parent (unless the child is five to seven years or older) or guardian regarding the child's ability to behave in an independent manner (Doll, 1947). The areas of maturity investigated are self-help (general), self-help (eating), self-help (dressing), self-direction, occupation, communication, locomotion, and socialization. It includes standard scores for a range of ages from birth to past the teenage years. It is adaptable for cross-cultural study. Responses to such questions such as those listed below are used to determine level of social independence or social age.

Walk about the room unattended (1 year level)
Cares for self at toilet (3+ year level)
Dresses self except tying (4+year level)

The Peabody Picture Vocabulary Test contains standard scores for ages two to eight years (Dunn, 1965). It is a test of comprehension involving vocabulary recognition. It proposes to measure verbal intelligence; however, since verbal ability involves more than comprehension, this is questionable. Since this test has been standardized on white children only and totally involves vocabulary, it is not adequate for cross-cultural study. For example, children from the state of Washington often identify the picture of a mountain range in response to the stimulus "cascade." In view of their proximity to the Cascade Mountain range this is logical; however, the "correct" response (according to the design of the test) is the picture of a waterfall. The Peabody has been widely used and is an adequate measure of standard vocabulary for ages four through twelve, although standardization scores cover a wider range. Above and below the ages four to twelve, reliability of measure decreases.

The Robbins Speech Sound Discrimination and Verbal Imagery Type Test is a test of auditory discrimination (Robbins and Robbins, 1966). It is used as a measure of the child's ability to discriminate the various speech sounds. Each initial presentation is accompanied by a picture reproduction. The child receives one point for each name that he can remember correctly when the corresponding picture plate is presented. There are pictures on each stimulus page with the pictures on the response page in random order but identical representations. Less familiar words and word-pairs may be omitted if the child is unable to memorize the names of the representative pictures. The preschool child's proficiency is measured by the percentage of correct responses.

The Templin-Darley Test of Articulation contains standardization scores for ages three to eight years (Templin and Darley, 1960). The child's proficiency in speech sound production on the McDonald Deep Test of Articulation is measured by the percent of correct responses (McDonald, 1964). Since articulation test measures presume a standard proficiency, the student is cautioned to take particular note of population used in the validation procedures. The Templin-Darley and McDonald are currently two of the most widely used tests of articulation. Both are designed to test the child's ability to produce sounds in words. The Templin is arranged in order of increasing complexity of production. The McDonald is arranged so that connected speech sound movement can be measured with the least amount of effort through the use of compound words such as "tub/nose," "house/sun" and "ball/lamp."

The Fisher-Logemann Test of Articulation Competence is one of the few articulation inventories that directs the examiner to account for dialect variations without penalty (Fisher and Logemann, 1971). It has been standardized on a cross-cultural population of five hundred children. Phonological rules for both the picture form and sentence form are delineated into five broad categories of native, geographical and class dialect variations including: General American, Eastern, New York City, Southern and Negro. This, of course, does not account for many of the other possible variations of a given population. However, the examiner is cautioned to be familiar with the dialect of the child before he makes assumptions about articulation competence. The sentence form is useful only if the subject can read. The picture form contains thirty-five items represented by large color illustrations. The test instructs the examiner to seek voluntary responses and to discourage imitation. The obvious value of this test is that proficiency is evaluated within the framework of the child's dialectal phonology; a framework that is "standard" for him.

The Berry-Talbot Exploratory Test of Grammar involves items that measure grammar and syntax responses for ages five to eight years (Berry and Talbot, 1966). It attempts to avoid the cultural influences of language by using nonsense words such as "nad," "lutz," "trop," and "bing." The items are designed to measure internalized rules of plurization, formation of verb tense, use of adjectives and personal pronouns. Each representation is accompanied by a representative nonsense picture of the figure. Normative scaled scores are not presented. The child's morphological proficiency is measured by predicting the rules of grammar that might be exhibited by an average child at each specific age level. Information is provided regarding the expected number of errors according to levels of morphological structure. The possibilities of this test might lie in its adaptability to cross-cultural studies. This is primarily because of its use of nonsense words and the absence of standardization of responses.

The Illinois Test of Psycholinguistic Abilities (ITPA 1968

Figure 16. Plate XVII from Berry-Talbot Exploratory Test of Grammar © 1966. (By permission of Mildred Berry, Rockford, Illinois.)

edition) contains standardization scores for ages 2.7 to 9.11 years (McCarthy and Kirk, 1968). It is divided into ten subtests involving auditory-vocal, and visual-motor responses. The child's ability to use these channels are measured at the receptive, expressive, and organizational levels. There are two supplementary subtests involving auditory-vocal responses that need not be administered in order to compute the psycholinguistic age level (PLA). Receptive level implies the ability to decode incoming visual and auditory information. Expressively, the child must demonstrate the ability to encode ideas manually (gesture) or verbally. Organization involves the ability to relate, organize and manipulate visual or auditory symbols. Information involving visual and auditory memory and closure (identification through anticipated responses) are measured at the automatic level.

Although this test has some distinct advantages over intelligence tests in measuring language skills, it has not been standardized on a cross-cultural basis. The Grammatic Closure subtest, for example, presumes standardized grammatic structure. The following example of plurization responses demonstrates this point:

> Here is a woman, here are two women–standard
> Here is a woman, here are two womens–dialect

As pointed out in the preceding chapter, the dialect sample above is as correct for a dialect system as the standard is for a standard system. The ITPA indicates that only the standard sample is correct. Although the Grammatic Closure subtest may be omitted when consistent phonological variation is present, other verbal subtests involve the standard/dialect dichotomy. Items involving visual stimuli, on the other hand, are more closely akin to items found in the listing of prelinguistic skills at the beginning of this chapter. In this respect, the visual items may provide a more adequate measure of abilities in cross-cultural studies than would the verbal items. As a measure of standard language development, this test provides a profile of areas of strength and weakness that are more directly related to language than other tests.

COMPREHENSIVE EVALUATION

The comprehensive measure of language skills should at first be concerned with the *tools* of language and then with the *functional* use of those tools. Does the child have the ability to produce language first? Can he hear sounds? Is he independent enough to experiment with sounds? Can he understand language? Has his development been "normal?" An audiologic evaluation and a talk with his mother about his activities at home will give you most of this information. The Vineland can be used for further exploration of social maturity (independence and experimentation). The Peabody Picture Vocabulary Test, as well as informal conversation, will yield clues to comprehensive ability. The child's degree of articulation proficiency can be observed through conversation or through a formal articulation inventory (such as the *Fisher-Logemann*), but the test scores may only indicate proficiency for certain word production rather than overall production.

Once the evaluator has some idea of the child's ability to produce language, the evaluation should be concerned with the degree of functional language. Since language is not *exclusively* verbal, the evaluation should not be exclusively verbal. Any of the aforementioned test instruments are applicable if the examiner remains cognizant of the limitations of test instruments.

A comprehensive evaluation of the child's overall development would include a number of tests that would measure *ability* without penalty. The child's ability to perform tasks involving cognitive and associative responses should be measured. This would include test instruments that use visual items as well as verbal items. Test responses should involve categorization, discrimination, rote and sequential memory. In addition, language and motor skills should be evaluated. Motor skill evaluation would be specifically directed toward assessment of fine motor coordination such as would be necessary for some speech sound movements. Language should be measured expressively and receptively. Language tests are by nature culturally bound so any attempts to measure language ability must be culture specific. This would, of course, involve adaptations of the present language test instruments. The child's ability to behave in an independent manner should be evaluated by investigating his personal-social behavior within the environment.

If a child is nonverbal, it does not imply that he has no language. It does imply that he lacks expressive language skills. If a child has difficulty completing visual discrimination items and appears to be socially immature, he may have expressive difficulties that are a result of these inabilities. If, however, his language is phonologically different from the standard this does not necessarily indicate a specific deficiency. The point here is that testing is not just the administration of the test but careful consideration of all pertinent data before conclusions are reached. Evaluation begins with complete knowledge of the test instrument and its applicability in determining developmental level (rather than proving deficit). It ends with the evaluators' knowledge of limited conclusions versus over generalizations. Somewhere in between, the child is subjected to a test battery by an examiner who tries *not* to represent the authority figure (in some instances this might mean changing examiners). Most important of all, the examiner must know what abilities he is looking for, what prerequisites are necessary to the development of these skills, and how the skills may be changed by environmental influences. The final chapter could be used as a guide to the overall development of the child to age five.

Chapter Nine

THE CHILD FROM BIRTH TO FIVE

THE child is a communicator although he has not developed an adult code of verbal behavior. His responsibilities as a speaker are as varied as they are for the adult. He perhaps relies on perceptual coding more than the adult, but as a communicator he is both speaker and listener.

In a relatively short period of time, the child recognizes that he can make sounds and begins to use those sounds for his own pleasure. His coos and gurgles in the crib are a personal experience. Very often mothers report that infants cease their vocalizations when an adult approaches the crib. As the child gains reinforcement(either internal pleasure of external stimulation), his vocalizations increase. He progresses from "ta-ta-li-la-boo" at the babbling stage to "baby sleep" to "dis my shoe" to "We play games at the park today" at a rapid pace. This progression is influenced and shaped by his experimentations and explorations into the world.

The child cannot gain the necessary skills for language without a great amount of experience and consistent experimentation. The ability is species-specific, while the skill is developmental and involves all areas of maturation: neurological, motor, and social. Before we can begin to understand the complexity of language, we must understand the importance of considering the overall structure of development.

The purpose of this chapter, then, is to review in one "fell swoop" the developmental progression of the child from birth to age five. This summary will include skills in the following areas: motor, (subcategory, fine motor coordination), visual perception, social awareness, play activity, listening and attention, adaptive and emotional, and speech and language behavior.

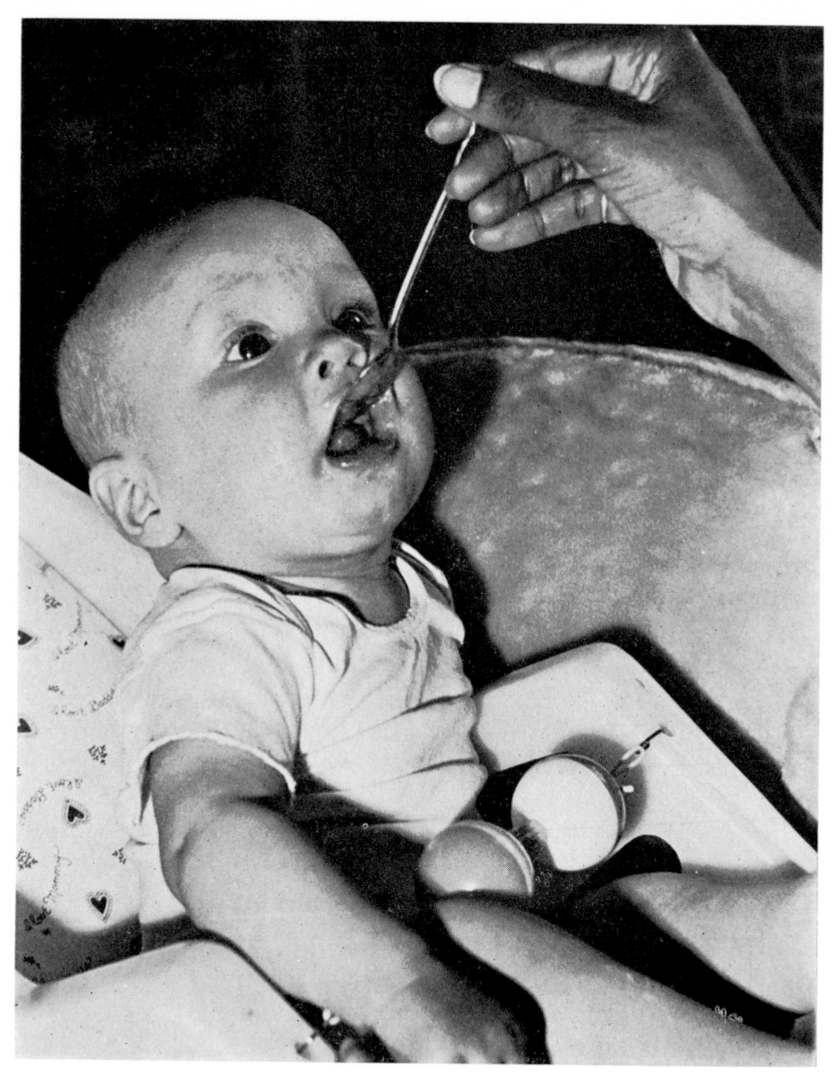

Sound production is often stimulated while the infant is eating. (Courtesy Wood Photographs)

BIRTH TO SIX MONTHS

In the first few weeks of life, the child is internally oriented. Motor skills are reflexive in nature. Initially, he sleeps, fifteen to twenty hours per day. Most vocalization involves crying and whimpering, although there is evidence of vowel behavior (most often back vowels). He is farsighted and cannot focus on one object.

The child at one to three months responds to strong external stimuli by crying. These sounds are used as a carrier of emotion in early child language (Jakobson, 1961). In other words, the child uses crying, whimpering, etc. as a way of indicating internal disorders and pleasures, since at this stage he is more concerned with hunger, sleep, and pain than he is with external stimulation. Front and middle vowels are more often produced in combination with such consonants as *m, n, p, t, d.* Although the child attends to sound, he is not yet a social being.

From six weeks to four months there is an increase in social awareness. He begins to laugh and coo and recognizes people (usually parents only). He vocalizes more appropriately, using mostly vowel sounds with intonation patterns. Motor development skills have progressed to that stage where he can hold his head erect and roll from back to side. Vocal "play" has increased. For example, the child may pass away the hours following the path of light made by a mobile hanging above the crib. Occasionally there may be a rather awkward attempt to reach it and sometimes with success but grasping skills have not developed as yet.

SIX MONTHS TO TWELVE MONTHS

From five to eight months, he smiles to gain attention. He has also cut his first tooth by this time. He can roll over and can grab objects although grasp techniques are still primitive. He begins to react to the environment consistently—he becomes a social being. He is delighted with his successes and responds to pleasure/displeasure outside of the hunger-pain cycle. He responds consistently to the human voice. All of the vowel sounds and most of the consonant sounds occur in his babbling activity. Deese (1970) states that, "If it (babbling) is developed and prolonged, the babbling acquires the stress and intonation patterns of meaningful speech." Most researchers regard babbling as a prelanguage stage where the child is experimenting with sounds and patterns of sounds.

From seven to ten months, the child explores through the

Figure 17. During the early years of socialization children may engage in parallel play rather than in cooperative play (after Camper).

sense of touch. Motor skills have developed rapidly. He begins to show some degree of selectiveness and individuality. He enjoys his sound productions and shows it by repeating sequences (either his own or stimulated ones)—echolalia. He listens to familiar words and toward the later end of this period, the first "word" may appear in the form of "mama," "tata," "dada," etc. He responds appropriately to simple verbal commands such as "no-no" by ceasing activity momentarily.

The child seeks affection, and there may be the emergence of creeping and crawling behavior. His vocalization behavior at "play" is echoic in nature. He repeats sounds (occurrence of "mama," etc.). He begins to "taste-test" new items.

The ten to twelve month old child is ambulatory. He pulls himself to a standing position and walks, although he sometimes needs help. If an object catches his immediate attention, he may resort to crawling for faster locomotion. He has said his first "word," and it is (by this time) usually recognizable to more than just the immediate members of the family. He reacts to tone of voice as well as special words such as "no," "bye-bye," etc. He has begun to develop the pincer grasp and may spend a great deal of time practicing (such as dropping items over the side of the table or playpen rail—distressing to adults by the fifteenth drop but an essential experiment for the child). The following would not be an unusual diary entry:

> Sunny learned to master her plosive sound in the middle of her peas. She had been trying for weeks, but when the spoon was removed from her lips, the sound just seemed to "pop" out (along with a few peas).

TWELVE TO EIGHTEEN MONTHS

The period from twelve to eighteen months is sometimes known as the "speech readiness period." It is during this time that the first words are clearly established. The beginnings of locomotor activity change his point of focus to the floor and the general environment and increase his need for language. However, speech activity may seem to lag for a period as he concentrates on motor activity. He begins to vocalize (utter some sort of sound) to indicate his wants. He is often confused by opposites (and mothers tend to issue a multitude of positive-negative directives as his locomotor activity increases). Gesell (1940) notes that ten to twelve words or more may be present.

The child has greater control over his movements. Chewing has improved and he experiments with the functions of things around him. He may flush the toilet endlessly or answer the telephone, chatter a few seconds and hang up before mother can arrive to rescue the caller. The child is usually delighted with his success during these experiments and may show very little concern for mother's consternation by turning his attention immediately to some other area. Friendships scarcely exist for a child of this age, and although he may engage in parallel play in the company of another child, there is relatively no sharing involved.

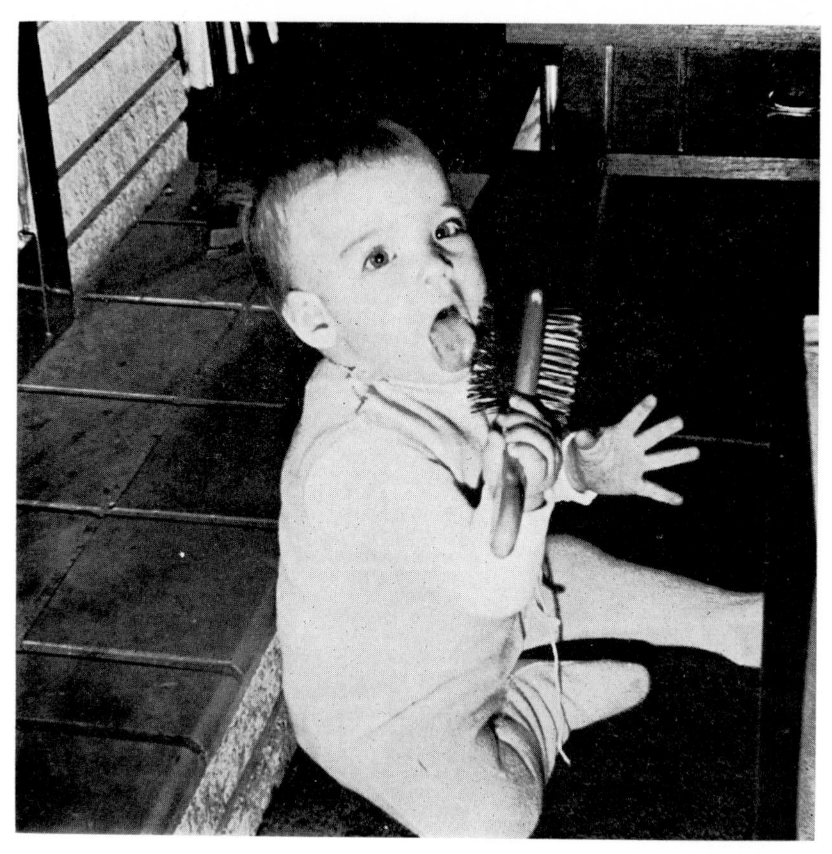

Although taste-testing helps the child catalog objects, it does tend to make adults nervous. (Courtesy Wood Photographs)

EIGHTEEN TO TWENTY-FOUR MONTHS

In the period from eighteen to twenty-four months, there is a spurt in verbal production. Two-word phrases that are descriptive and meaningful may begin. Piaget (1970) notes that egocentric speech activity is initiated during this period. Most of the utterances involve naming behavior. In Smith and Miller (1966) it is noted that the vocabularly count reaches seventy-two words or more.

The child becomes selective in the way his needs will be satisfied. He is independent in spurts with periods of accentuated clinging. His motor activity improves as well. He tries throwing a ball, uses a cup and spoon consistently, and his balance has improved greatly. During this period, there is a "thunderstorm" of motor activity. The child inspects everything and has learned to put on and take off covers, turn doorknobs, etc. It is during this time that doctors get frantic calls from mothers after the child has devoured something not usually classified under edible. I, for example, made such a phone call when I discovered that the contents of a bottle of Mr. Clean © had found its way into my youngest child's stomach. A more passive mode of behavior also develops at this period (thankfully!). The child begins to enjoy listening to simple stories when there are pictures involved.

TWO TO THREE YEARS

From the ages of two to three years, the child becomes more demanding. He is confused by a disruption of the household routine and appears to need the security of a schedule. He is explosively energetic and temper tantrums may easily occur. Pivot-open phrase utterances will increase, and about two-thirds of his utterances are intelligible. He obeys verbal commands and throughly enjoys a bedtime story.

Motor behavior now involves dancing, clapping, stamping during play. Facial expressions are more evident. Sphincter muscles have developed allowing toilet training to be successful. Eating involves more independence. He has most of his temporary teeth. He can discriminate and match shapes as well as identify pictures and actions. Dramatic play (role play) is more evident. The child may also have an imaginary playmate. At this age the following diary entry would not be unusual:

> Sunny often verbalizes and when she does it is sometimes difficult to understand her. She answers questions readily with two word phrases. She can identify the function of an object such as an airplane. She plays imaginatively but does not offer an explanation for her activity. For example, "No more bacakset. Wagon go boom?" When she sees the picture of a ribbon, she responds, "Oh, Honey!" and fondly touches her hair.

THREE TO FOUR YEARS

The ages of three to four years are known as the "chatterbox" years. The child seems to have doubled his inquisitive powers

All learning does not occur with commercial toys; every experience offers a learning situation. (Courtesy Wood Photographs)

and he enjoys being the center of attention. He also enjoys new and special words. He is able to repeat (although not often accurately) short rhymes and stories, and will do so with little provocation when it is least wanted. Lenneberg (1966) states that by thirty-six months the child has a vocabulary of 1000 words or more, consisting of four or five word phrases during conversational speech. His comprehension of "logical" material is often distorted. He appears to be more aggressive, but this is more indicative of attempts at adjustment and subsequent confusion than real aggression. He is rather possessive and demand-

The child experiments with language through role playing. (Courtesy Wood Photographs)

ing. He may insist on stories being retold or reread word for word. Concern is expressed by staring at another in distress or by putting an arm around the suffering friend and saying, "Does it hurt?" He is concerned about routine. His sleep hours have decreased and his sleep schedule is established.

Motorically, he is able to stand on one foot, leap off the floor with feet together, and can ascend and descend steps or a ladder. He is able to use a tricycle or wagon, toss and catch a ball. The first permanent teeth may begin to erupt. The child can feed himself without spilling food, and dress himself except for tying and buttoning. He may reverse shoes to the wrong foot, but he is able to complete the major job of dressing. He can also wash and dry his own hands. Although he takes the responsibility for toilet activities (and announces his intentions), he may wait too long to finally get there.

His play activities are very repetitive. Social play is almost incidental and solitary play is still characteristic. He can turn the pages of a book, reciting a story from the pictures. Shape discrimination has improved.

This is a child who might recite his own version of "Twinkle Twinkle Little Star" repeatedly, or announce when he is ready to leave during a visit. This is also the child who will begin to ask the "impossible" question but who is not interested in a complicated or complex answer (indeed, he often seems not to be interested in any answer at all).

FOUR TO FIVE YEARS

The child becomes less recalcitrant from the ages of four to five years, but at the same time his need to gain information often prompts parents to run for the nearest encyclopedia. Ninety percent of his speech is intelligible. His vocabulary has tripled, and his phrase units are more complex. He begins to understand a word independent of the inflection in which it is spoken and the context in which it occurs. He begins to be concerned about future events and he used speech to fit himself into "the scheme of things."

Since the child may have some difficulty finding the "right" word, his speech is usually of high emotional content, and he is more ego-involved in his output. Some "hesitations and blocking" may be associated with stressful speech situations. He tends to change the subject rapidly and expresses limitations ("I can't," "No") and conformation ("I can do it myself," "Is that right?"). He tells the function rather than the name and elaborates about details. Soon the pivot-open class distinction will no longer suffice as a method of describing his linguistic units.

The child at this age has a tendency to boast, brag, tattle, and quarrel. He is fascinated with "naughty" words. Although he is highly tuned to social boundaries, he may be unable to operate within them. He can take on responsible chores, and

The four-year-old is ready to assume responsibilities. (Courtesy Wood Photographs)

tries to go beyond the boundaries of parental authority. His imagination is limitless. He fantasizes on a personal basis and relates his fantasies as truth. He begins to enjoy other children and takes a more active role in competitive games (although the rules are followed with some difficulty). He may have a special friend.

The four-to-five-year-old has some perception of time and space. He can draw a picture that includes some details and is relatively imitative of the environment. Cows may be green or people may fail to have bodies, but the child sticks to the details that are important to him and incorporates his imagination into the picture. He may be able to count objects to less than five, while counting by rote may be expanded to ten. Memory for rote counting far exceeds his knowledge of one-to-one concepts and "more or less' concepts. He works hard at solving manipulative tasks such as copying a square or triangle, lacing shoes (he still cannot tie them), using crayons, and trying to use scissors although the latter item is usually unsuccessful. Motorically, he can skip on one foot, climbs stairs in an alternative fashion, climbs as high as permitted (trees, etc.), throws overhand, and likes balancing activities. Role playing takes up a great deal of time and planning. Items are used with purpose; for example, chopping paper for rice, arranging flat rocks for meat, and washing leaves for a salad. Roles are clearly defined: "You be the mommy, I'll be the daddy."

FIVE TO SIX YEARS

The child from five to six begins to organize information. He classifies under "who" and "what" and has a consistent use of pronouns and other grammatical parts of speech. He enjoys telling stories. He begins to produce blends but still may have some difficulty with *th, r and l.*

He takes excursions into the neighborhood and may become interested in purchasing items from the store. He likes to make things and experiment with materials. He is able to participate in competitive activities, taking turns and keeping score. The concept of time is related to everyday experiences as well as holidays. He can hit a ball with a stick, kick the ball with more accuracy, use scissors more effectively, and dramatize stories.

He begins to use expressions such as, "I thought . . ., I forgot . . ., Can I? . . ." His sentence structure becomes more efficient and indicative of underlying structures. He becomes more adapt at handling abstract information. He clearly has knowledge (and is more than willing to prove it although there may be times when the security of home is more inviting than the formidable outside world of strangers). For example, "I want to go to school. Where will you be when I'm at school, mommy?"

The child has become a communicator. He can absorb complex ideas and is quite capable of functioning as an independent

The end of the preschool years marks the beginning of independence. (Courtesy Wood Photographs)

individual in terms of language. Although he will develop more and more complex language patterns he has the basic essentials of his native language system. He has developed listening skills, social skills, motor skills, and perceptual skills. He will continue to use these skills to expand his language system. He has learned through experimentation and practice that this (innate ability) will help him catalog his world and bring order out of chaos. Language serves to bring similarities and differences into focus so that he may deal with his perceptions and his ever expanding world.

What this book has attempted to do, then, is to provide the

beginning student of speech and language development with a brief description of the child from birth through age five. It contains normative data, but normative data should always be considered a checklist of behavior, not an absolute compendium of facts. The child's progression through those years depends on his needs and on the variety of experiences offered him by the environment. He can proceed no faster than his last level of maturation and no faster than the opportunity to gain skill at another level. "The role of development is not constant during the formative years, and there may be transient slowing in the rate of maturation with subsequent hastening" (Lennebrg, 1966).

In order for language to be functional, a child should expand his world both physically and mentally. If the environment does not allow experimentation, then language will be hampered. "The retarding factor for language acquisition here must be a psychological one or perhaps a cognitive one . . ." (Lenneberg, 1966). The child gears his language to his needs. Those needs are set by the events and relationships with a particular group of people within a particular culture. He develops a dialect that is set by the culture and the home. If language reflects his needs and his cultural background, it is adequate. Speak *to* the child, not *at* the child. It is his language, not yours, that will be "the horse to carry him into a far country."

BIBLIOGRAPHY

Ainsfeld, Moshe, Bogo, N., and Lambert, W. E.: Evaluation reactions to accented English speech. *J Abnorm Soc Psychol, 65:*223-231, 1962.

Ainsfeld, Moshe and Carlson, Patricia: Some observations in the linguistic competence of a two year old child. *Child Dev. 40:*569-575, 1969.

Ainsfeld, Moshe and Tucker, R. G.: English pluralization rules of six year old children. *Child Dev. 38:*1202-1217, 1967.

Alyeshmerni, M., and Taubr, P.: *Working with Aspects of Language.* New York, Harcourt, Brace and World, 1970.

Anastasi, Anne: *Psychological Testing,* 3rd ed., New York, Macmillan, 1961.

Anastasi, Anne, and deJesus, C.: Language development and nonverbal IQ of Puerto Rican preschool children in New York City. *J Abnorm Soc Psychol, 48:*357-366, 1953.

Anderson, Ruth, Miles, M., and Mathney, P.: *Communicative Evaluation Chart from Infancy to Five Years.* Golden Colorado Business Forms, Inc., 1964.

Bannatyne, Alex: A comparison of visuo-spatial and visuo-motor memory for designs and their relationship to other sensori-motor psycholinguistic variables. *J Learn Disabils, 2:*451-466, 1969.

Bar-Adon, A., and Leopold, W.: *Child Language: A Book of Readings.* Englewood Cliffs, New Jersey, Prentice-Hall, 1971.

Baratz, Joan: Teaching reading in an urban Negro school system. In Fredrick Williams (Ed.): *Language and Poverty: Perspectives on a Theme,* Inst. for Res. on Pov. Monogr. Ser. Chicago, Markham Pub. Co., 11-24, 1970.

——— Should Black children learn white dialect? *ASHA,* September 1970, 415-417.

——— A bi-dialectal task for determining language proficiency in economically disadvantaged Negro children. *Child Dev. 40:*889-901, 1969.

——— Linguistic and cultural factors in teaching reading to ghetto children. *Elem English, 46:*199-203, 1969.

——— Language in the economically disadvantaged child: A perspective. *ASHA, 10:*143-45, 1968.

Bateman, Barbara: *Interpretations of the 1961 Illinois Test of Psycholinguistic Abilities.* Seattle, Special Child Publications, 1968.

——— *The Illinois Test of Psycholinguistic Abilities in Current Research.* Urbana, Institute for Research on Exceptional Children, University of Illinois, April 1964.

Battin, R.: Two methods of presenting information on speech and language development. *J Speech Hrng Disords, 27:*17-22, 1962.

Bellugi, Ursula: Learning the Language. *Psychol Today,* 32-35, January, 1970.

Benninghoff/Goerttler: *Lehrbuch der Anatomie des Menschen, II.* Band: Eingeweide und Kreislauf. 9. Auflage von Helmut Ferner. Urban & Schwarzenberg München-Berlin-Wien 1971.

Bereiter, C. and Engleman, S.: *Teaching the Disadvantaged Child in the Preschool.* New Jersey, Prentice-Hall, 1966.

Berko, Jean: The child's learning of English morphology. *Word, 14:*150-177, 1958.

Bernstein, Basil: Language and social class. *Brit J Socio. 11:*271-76, 1960.

——— A sociolinguistic approach to socialization: with some reference to educability. In Fredrick Williams (Ed.) *Language and Poverty: Perspectives on a Theme,* Inst. for Res on Pov. Monogr. Ser. Chicago, Markham Publishing Co., 1970.

Berry, Mildred: *Language Disorders in Children: The Bases and Diagnosis.* New York, Meredith Corp., Appleton Century Crofts, 1969.

Berry, Mildred and Eisenson, Jon: *Speech Disorders: Principles and Procedures of Therapy.* New York, Meredith Corp., 1956.

Berry, Mildred, and Talbot, R.: *Exploratory Test of Grammar.* 4332 Pine Crest Rd., Rockford, Ill., 61107, 1966.

Blomquist, B. L.: Diadochokinetic movement of nine-, ten-, and eleven-year-old children. *J Spch Hrng Disords, 15:*159-164, 1950.

Bloom, Lois: Why pivot grammar. *J Spch Hrng Disords, 36:*40-49, 1971.

Bloomfield, Leonard: *Language.* New York, Holt, 1933.

——— Literate and illiterate speech. *American Speech, 2:*430-439, 1927.

——— A set of postulates for the science of language. *Language, 2:* 1926.

Braine, M. D. S.: The otongeny of English phrase structure: the first phase. *Language, 39:*1-13, 1963.

——— The acquisition of language in infant and child. In Carol Reed (Ed.): *The Learning of Language: Essays in Honor of David H. Russell.* New York, Appleton-Century Crofts, 1970.

Bram, J.: *Language and Society.* New York, Random House, 1955.

Brammon, J.: A comparison of syntactic structures in the speech of three and four year old children. *Lang Spch, 11:*171-181, 1968.

Brisbane, Holly: Speech development before the first year. In *The Developing Child.* Peoria, Ill., Bennett, 1965, 164-67.

——— Speech development: three to six years. In *The Developing Child.* Peoria, Ill., Bennett, 1965, 333-36.

Brown, Charles, and Van Riper, Charles: *Speech and Man.* New Jersey, Prentice-Hall, 1966.

Brown, Claude: The language of soul. *Esquire,* 69: April 1968.

Brown, Roger: *Psycholinguistics: Selected Papers.* New York, Free Press, 1970.

——— *Words and Things*. New York, Free Press, 1958.

Brown, Roger, and Bellugi, Ursula: Three processes in the child's acquisition of syntax. *Harv. Educal. Rev, 34:*133-151, 1964.

Brown, Roger, and Bellugi, Ursula (Eds.): The acquisition of language. Monog. Soc. Res. in Child Dev, *29:* #92, 101-107, 1964.

Bruner, Jerome: On cognitive growth. In John Eliot (Ed.): *Human Development and Cognitive Processes*. New York, Holt Rinehart and Winston, 1971, 322-357.

Bruner, Jerome: Eye, hand and mind. In D. Elkind and J. Flavell (Eds.): *Studies in Cognitive Development: Essays in Honor of Jean Piaget*. New York, Oxford Univ. Press, 1969, 223-236.

Bunker, Robert: *Other Men's Skies*. Bloomington, Ind., University Press, 1956.

Burks, A., and Guilford, P.: Wakulla County oral language project. *Elem English, 46:*606-611, 1969.

Bzoch, Kenneth and League, Richard: *Receptive Expressive Emergent Language Scale for the Measurement of Language Skills in Infancy* (Reel). Gainesville, Florida, Computer Management Corp., 1971.

Carpenter, C.: Patterns of language used by kindergarten children. *Volta Rev, 68:*606-611, 1969.

Carr, Josephine: Investigations of the spontaneous speech sounds of five year old deafborn children. *J Spch Hrng Disords, 18:*22-29, 1953.

Carrow, Sister Mary: Linguistic functioning of bilingual and monolingual children. *J Spch Hrng Disords 22:*371-380, 1957.

Cattell, R. B.: A culture free intelligence test. *J Educ Psychol, 3:*161-80, 1940.

Cattell, R. B., Feinfold, S., and Sarrason, S.: A culture free intelligence test: II, an evaluation of cultural influences on test performances. *J Educ Psychol, 32:*81-100, 1941.

Cazden, Courtney: Neglected situations in child language: research and education. In Fredrick Williams (Ed.): *Language and Poverty: Perspectives on a Theme,* Inst. Res. Pov. Monogr. Ser. Chicago, Markham Publishing Company, 1970, 81-101.

Cazden, Courtney: Studies of early language acquisition. *Child Educ, 46:* 127-131, 1969.

——— On individual differences in language competence and performance. *J Spec Educ, 1:*135-150, 1967.

Chomsky, Carol: *The Acquisition of Syntax in Children from Five to Ten*. Res. Monog. No. 57, Cambridge, Mass., MIT Press, 1969.

Chomsky, Noam: Three models for the description of language. In Alfred Smith (Ed.): *Communication and Culture*. New York, Holt Rinehart and Winston, 140-151.

——— *Aspects of the Theory of Language*. Cambridge, Mass., MIT Press, 1965.

——— *Syntactic Structures.* The Hague, Mouton Press, 1957.

Church, Joseph: *Language and The Discovery of Reality.* New York, Random House, 1961.

Clark, A., and Richards, C.: Auditory discrimination among economically disadvantaged and nondisadvantaged preschool children. *Except Child, 33:*259-262, 1966.

Cohn, W. On the language of lower class children. *Sch Rev 67:*435-440, 1959.

Cooper, June: Training of teachers of speech for the economically disadvantaged Black American student. *West Spch, 34:*139-143, 1970.

Cousins, Norman: The Environment of Language. *Sat Rev,* p. 36, April 1967.

Critchley, E. M. R.: Reversals in language: the importance of kinesthetic feedback mechanisms. *J Learn Disabils, 1:*722-25, 1968.

Cromer, R.: The development of temporal reference during the acquisition of language. Unpub. doctoral dissertation, Harvard Univ. 1968.

Darley, F., and Winitz, H.: Age of the first word: review of research. *J Spch Hrng Disords, 26:*272-90, 1961.

Davis, Lawrence: Social dialectology in America: a critical survey. *J Eng Linguistics, 4:*46-56, 1970.

Day, E.: The development of language in twins. In Wayne Dennis (Ed.) *Readings in Child Psychology.* New York, Prentice Hall, 179-99, 360-68, 1963.

Deese, James: *Psycholinguistics.* Boston, Allyn and Bacon, 1970.

Deutsch, Cynthia: The role of social class in language development and cognition. *Amer J Orthopsych, 25:*78-88, 1965.

——— Auditory discrimination and learning: social factors. *Merill-Palmer Quart, 10:*277-96, 1964.

DeVito, Joseph: *The Psychology of Speech and Language: An Introduction to Psycholinguistics.* New York, Random House, 1970.

Doll, Edgar A.: *Vineland Social Maturity Scale.* Minneapolis, Educational Testing Bureau, 1947.

——— *The Oseretsky Tests of Motor Proficiency.* Minneapolis, Educational Testing Bureau, 1946.

Dove, Adrian: Soul story. *New York Times Magazine, 82:* December 1968.

Dove, Adrian: Black questions for Whitey. *Time Magazine, 40:* July 1968.

Dunn, H. A.: Communication and purpose: ingredients for longevity. *J Spch Disords, 26:*109-177, 1961.

Dunn, L.: *The Peabody Picture Vocabulary Test.* Minneapolis, American Guidance Service, 1965.

Ecroyd, D., Halfond, M., and Towne, C.: *Voice and Articulation: A Handbook.* Glenview, Illinois, Scott Foresman and Co., 1966.

Eisenberg, L., Berlin, C., Dell, A., and Sheldon, F.: Class and race effects on the intelligibility of nonsense syllables. *Child Dev, 34:*1077-1089, 1963.

Eliot, John: *Human Development and Cognitive Processes.* New York, Holt, Rinehart and Winston, 1971.

Elkind, D.: Conservation and concept formation. In D. Elkind and J. Flavell (Eds.): *Studies in Cognitive Development: Essays in Honor of Jean Piaget.* New York, Oxford Univ. Press, 1969, 171-190.

Ellingson, Careth: *The Shadow Children.* Chicago, Professional Press, 1967.

Elliott, C. H.: *Textbook of the Nervous System.* Philadelphia, J. B. Lippincott Co., 1947.

Engleman, S.: How to construct effective language programs for the poverty child. In Fredrick Williams (Ed.): *Language and Poverty: Perspectives on a Theme,* Instit. Res. Pov. Monogr. Ser. Chicago, Markham Pub. Co., 1970, 102-22.

Entwisle, Doris: Semantic systems of children: some assessments of social class and ethnic differences. In Fredrick Williams (Ed.) *Language and Poverty: Perspectives on a Theme.* Instit. Res. Pov. Monogr. Ser., Chicago, Markham Pub. Co., 1970, 123-39.

——— Developmental sociolinguistics: inner city children. *Amer J Sociol, 74:*37-49, 1968.

Entwisle, Doris, and Greenberger, Ellen: Racial difference in the language of grade school children. *Sociol Educ, 42:*238-250, 1969.

Ervin-Tripp, Susan: Discourse of argument: how children answer questions. In John Hayes (Ed.): *Cognition and the Development of Language.* New York, John Wiley and Sons, 1970, 79-108.

Fanon, Frantz: *Black Skin White Masks.* New York, Grove Press, 1967.

Festinger, Leon: *A Theory of Cognitive Dissonance.* Evanston, Row/Peterson, 1957.

Fisher, Hilda and Logemann, J.: *Therapist's Manual for the Fisher-Logemann Test of Articulation Competence.* Boston, Houghton-Mifflin, 1971.

Fishman, Joshua: *Sociolinguistics: A Brief Introduction.* Rowley, Mass., Newbury House Pub., 1970.

Fletcher, S.: Speech as an element in organization of a motor response. *J Hear Res, 5:*292-300, 1962.

Furth, Hans: *Piaget and Knowledge: Theoretical Foundations.* Englewood Cliffs, New Jersey, Prentice Hall, 1969.

Gardner, E. *Fundamentals of Neurology.* Philadelphia, W. B. Saunders Co., 1947.

Gesell, A.: The total action system: language. In *Infant Development: The Embryology of Early Human Behavior.* New York, Harper, 1952, 6-10.

Gesell, A.: *The First Five Years of Life: A Guide to the Study of the Preschool Child.* New York, Harper, 1940.

Gesell, A., and Armatruda, C.: *Developmental Diagnosis: Normal and Abnormal Child Development.* New York, Paul C. Hoeber Inc., 1941.

Gesell, A., and Ilg, F.: *The Child From Five to Ten.* New York, Harper, 1949.

Gleason, H. A.: *An Introduction to Descriptive Linguistics.* New York, Holt Rinehart and Winston, 1961.

Gleason, Patrick, and Wakefield, Nancy (Eds.): *Language and Culture.* Columbus, Ohio, C. E. Merrill, 1968.

Goldstein, Kurt: *Language and Language Disturbances.* New York, Grune and Stratton, 1948.

Goodenough, Florence, Maurer, K., and Van Wagenen, M.: *Minnesota Preschool Scales.* Minneapolis, Educational Testing Bureau, 1932-1940.

Goodman, Kenneth: On valuing diversity in language. *Child Educ, 46:* 1969.

Goodnow, J.: Problems in research on culture and thought. In D. Elkind and J. Flavell (Eds.): *Studies in Cognitive Development: Essays in Honor of Jean Piaget.* New York, Oxford Univ. Press, 1969, 439-464.

Gordon, P.: *Baby Learning Through Baby Play: A Parent's Guide for the First Two Years.* New York, St. Martins Press, 1970.

Graham, N. C.: Memory span and language proficiency. *J Learn Disabils, 1:*644-48, 1968.

Gray, G., and Wise, C.: *The Bases of Speech.* New York, Harper and Bros., 1959.

Greenberg, J. H. (Ed.): *Universals of Language.* Cambridge Mass., M.I.T. Press, 1963.

Hadding-Koch, Kerstin: Some problems in psycholinguistics. *Studia Linguistica, 22:*1-14, 1969.

Hall, Elizabeth: A conversation with Jean Piaget and Barbel Inhelder on how children learn. *Psychol Today,* May 1970, 125-132.

Halowinsky, Ivan: Seriation actions in preschool children. *J Learn. Disabils, 3:*457-58, 1970.

Harms, L. S.: Listener comprehension of speakers of three status groups. *Lang Spch, 4:*109-29, 1961.

Hayes, John R.: *Cognition and the Development of Language.* New York, Wiley, 1970.

Hebb, D. O.: *The Organization of Behavior.* New York, Wiley, 1949.

——— Concerning Imagery. *Psychol Rev, 75:*466-77, 1968.

Hess, R., and Shipman, V.: Early experience and the socialization of cognitive modes in children. In Donna Gelfand (Ed.): *Social Learning in Childhood: Readings in Theory and Application.* Belmont, Calif., Brooks/Cole Pub. Co., 1969, 295-311.

Hobson, Arline: Systematic language modeling. *Contemp Educ, 40:*225-227, 1969.

Holland, Audrey: Comment on language deficiency of disadvantaged children. *J Spch Hear Res, 13:*440-42, 1971.

Holt, G.: The ethno-linguistic approach to speech language learning. *Spch Teacher, 20:*98-100, 1970.

Houston, Susan: The study of language: trends and positions. In John Eliot (Ed.): *Human Development and Cognitive Processes.* New York, Holt, Rinehart and Winston, 1971, 256-82.

——— A reexamination of some assumptions about the language of the disadvantaged child. *Child Develpm, 41:*947-63, 1970.

——— A diachronic examination of linguistic universals. *ASHA, 10:*247-49, 1968.

Huffman, V.: Language learning at Rough Rock. *Child Educ, 40:*139-45, 1969.

Huffman, V., and McReynolds, L.: Auditory sequence learning in children. *J Spch Hear Res, 11:*179-88, 1969.

Hutt, M., and Gibby, Robert: Early childhood: the preschool years. In *The Child: Development and Adjustment.* Boston, Allyn and Bacon, 1959.

Huttenlocher, Janellen: Children's ability to order and orient objects. *Child Dev, 38:*1169-77, 1967.

——— Children's intellectual development. *J Educl Res, 59:*114-16, 1965.

Hymes, Dell, (Ed.): *Language in Culture and Society.* New York, Harper and Row, 1964.

Inhelder, B.: Memory and intelligence in the child. In D. Elkind and J. Flavell (Eds.): *Studies in Cognitive Development: Essays in Honor of Jean Piaget.* New York, Oxford Univ. Press, 1969, 337-64.

Irwin, Orvis C.: Infant speech: consonantal positions. *J Spch Hrng Disords, 16:*159-61, 1951.

——— Infant speech: development of vowel sounds. *J Spch Hrng Disords, 13:*31-34, 1948.

Irwin, Orvis C.: Infant speech: consonant sounds according to manner of articulation. *J Spch Hrng Disords, 12:*173-76, 397-404, 1947.

Jakobson, Roman: *Child Language.* Aphasia and Phonological Universals, The Hague, Mouton, 1968 (translation of Kindersprache, Aphasie und Allgemeine Lautgesetze. Uppsala: Almquist & Wiksell, 1941).

——— *Collected Works.* The Hague, Mouton and Co., 1963.

Jensen, Arthur: How much can we boost IQ and scholastic achievement?. *Harv Educal Rev, 39:*1-123, 1969.

John, Vera, and Horner, V.: Bilingualism and the Spanish speaking child. In Fredrick Williams (Ed.): *Language and Poverty: Perspectives on a Theme.* Inst. Res. on Pov. Monogr. Ser. Chicago, Markham Pub. Co., 1970, 140-152.

Johnson, D., and Myklebust, H.: *Learning Disabilities: Educational Principles and Practices.* New York, Grune and Stratton, 1967.

Johnson, Kenneth: *Teaching the Disadvantaged.* Palo Alto, Calif., Sci. Res. Assts. Inc., 1970.

Jones, John Charles: *Learning.* New York, Harcourt Brace and World, 1967, 84-92.

Joynt, D., and Cambourne, B.: Psycholinguistic development and the control of behavior. *Brit J Educl Psychol, 38:*249-260, 1968.

Kagen, Jerome, and Massen, Paul: Language. In *Child Development and Personality.* New York, Harper and Row, 1963.

Kagen, Jerome, and Kagen, N.: Individuality and cognitive performance. In Paul Mussen (Ed.): Carmichael's *Manual of Child Development.* New York, John Wiley & Sons, 1970, 1273-1365.

Kaplan, E., and Kaplan, G.: The Prelinguistic Child. In John Eliot (Ed.): *Human Development and Cognitive Processes.* New York, Holt Rinehart and Winston, 1971, 258-80.

Kaplan, R. B.: Cultural thought pattern in inter-cultural education. *Language Learning, 16:*1-20, 1966.

Kappleman, M.: A study of learning disorders among disadvantaged children. *J Learn Disabils, 2:*262-68, 1969.

Karelitz, Samuel, *et. al.:* Relation of crying activity in early infancy to speech and intellectual development at age three. *Child Dev, 35:*769-77, 1964.

Karlin, I. W., Karlin, D. B., and Gurren, L.: *Development and Disorders of Speech in Childhood.* Springfield, Thomas, 1965.

Klingbeil, G. M.: Historical background of the modern speech clinic: part two, aphasia. *J Spch Hrng Disords, 4:*267-84, 1939.

Koch, Sigmund: Sibling influence on childrens speech. *J Spch Hrng Disords, 21:*322-28, 1956.

Kochman, T.: "Rapping" in the Black ghetto. *Transaction, 6:*26-34, 1969.

Koffa, Kurt: Ideational learning problems in speaking and thinking. In *The Growth of the Mind: An Introduction to Child Psychology.* New York, Harcourt Brace and World, 1931, 319-31.

Kohlberg, Lawrence: Early educational cognitive development view. *Child Dev, 39:*1013-62, 1968.

Labov, W.: The logic of nonstandard English. In Fredrick Williams (Ed.): *Language and Poverty: Perspectives on a Theme.* Inst. Res. on Pov. Monogr. Ser. Chicago, Markham Pub. Co., 1970, 153-89.

——— *Social Stratification of English in New York City.* Washington, D.C., Center for Applied Linguistics, 1966.

——— Stages in the acquisition of standard English. In R. Shuy (Ed.): *Social Dialects and Language Learning.* Champaign, Ill., NCTE, 1965.

LaCivita, Alice, Kean, J., and Yamamota, K.: Socio-economic status of children and acquisition of grammar. *J Educl Res, 60:*71-74, 1966.

Langacker, R. W.: *Language and its Structure.* New York, Harcourt Brace and World, 1968.

Lawton, Denis: *Social Class, Language and Education.* London, Routledge, 1968.

Lee, Laura: A screening test for syntax development. *J Spch Hrng Disords, 35:*103-12, 1970.

——— Developmental sentence types: a method for comparing normal and deviant syntactic development. *J Spch Hrng Disords, 31*:311-30, 1966.

Lee, Richard: Preliminaries to language intervention. *Quart J Spch, 41*: 270-76, 1970.

Leiter, R. G. *Manual for the Leiter International Performance Scale*. Los Angeles, Calif., West. Psychol. Servs., 1950.

Lennenberg, Eric. *Biological Foundations of Language*. New York, Wiley, 1967.

——— The natural history of language. In F. Smith and G. Miller (Eds.): *The Genesis of Language: A Psycholinguistic Approach*. Cambridge, Mass., MIT Press, 1966, 219-52.

——— (Ed.) *New Directions in the Study of Language*. Cambridge, Mass., MIT Press, 1964.

Leopold, Werner: *Speech Development of a Bilingual Child: A Linguist's Record, Vols. 1-4*. Evanston, Ill., N.W. Univ. Press, 1949.

Levenstein, P., and Sunley, R.: Stimulation of verbal interaction between disadvantaged mothers and children. *Amer J Psychiat, 38*:116-21, 1968.

Lewis, M. M.: Expressive nature of early vocalizations. In Wayne Dennis (Ed.): *Readings in Child Psychology*. Englewood Cliffs, N. J., Prentice Hall, 1963, 149-58.

——— *Language Thought and Personality in Infancy and Childhood*. New York, Basic Books, 1963.

——— *Infant Speech: A Study of the Beginnings of Speech*. New York, Humanities Press, 1951.

Lloyd, D. J.: Our national mania for correctness. In P. Gleason and N. Wakefield (Eds.): *Language and Culture*. Columbus, Ohio, C. E. Merrill, 1968, 194-200.

Lundeen, Dale J.: Relationship of diadochokinesis to various speech sounds. *J Spch Hrng Disords, 15*:54-59, 1950.

Luria, Alexander, and Yudovich, F.: *Speech and the Development of Mental Processes in the Child*. London, Staples Press, 1959.

Lyons, John: *Introduction to Theoretical Linguistics*. London, Cambridge Univ. Press, 1968.

Macrorie, Ken: *Telling Writing*. New York, Hayden Book Co., 1970.

Marquart, D. I., and Bailey, L. I.: An evaluation of the culture free test of intelligence. *J Genet Psychol, 86*:353-58, 1955.

McCarthy, Dorothea, and Kirk, S.: *Manual for the Illinois Test of Psycholinguistic Abilities*. Urbana, Ill., Univ. of Illinois Press, 1968.

McCarthy, Dorothea: Language development in children. In L. Carmichael (Ed.): *Manual of Child Psychology*. New York, Wiley, 1954, 476-581.

McCurry, Wm., and Irwin, O. C.: A study of word appproximations in spontaneous speech of infants. *J Spch Hrng Disords, 18*:133-39, 1953.

McDavid, Raven: The cultural matrix of American English. *Elem English, 42*:13-21, 1965.

McDonald, Eugene T.: *The Deep Test of Articulation.* Pittsburgh, Stanwix House Inc., 1964.

McNeill, David: *The Acquisition of Language: The Study of Developmental Psycholinguistics.* New York, Harper and Row, 1970.

——— Developmental psycholinguistics. In F. Smith and G. Miller (Eds.): *The Genesis of Language: A Psycholinguistic Approach.* Cambridge, Mass., MIT Press, 1966, 15-80.

Meader, Mary: The effect of disturbances in the developmental processes upon emergent specificity of function. *J Spch Hrng Disords, 5:*211-219, 1940.

Mehler, J., and Bluer, T.: Cognitive capacity of very young children. In Donna Gelfand (Ed.): *Social Learning in Childhood: Readings in Theory and Application.* Belmont, Calif., Brooks/Cole Pub. Co., 1969, 263-68.

Menyuk, Paula: Language theories and educational practices. In Fredrick Williams (Ed.): *Language and Poverty: Perspectives on a Theme.* Instit. Res. on Pov. Monog. Ser. Chicago, Markham Pub. Company, 1970, 190-211.

——— *Sentences Children Use.* Cambridge, Mass., MIT Press, 1969.

Meyers, Russell: Aphasia shortcourse, unpublished papers. Wichita, Kan., Instit. Logopedics, July 1950.

Mickelson, N., and Gallaway, C.: Cumulative language deficit among Indian children. *Except Child, 36:*187-90, 1969.

Miller, W., and Ervin, S.: The development of grammar in child language. In R. Brown and U. Bellugi (Eds.): The Acquisition of Language, Monog. Soc. Res. in Child Dev, 29:9-34, 1964.

Monsees, Edna, and Berman, Carol: Speech and language screening in a summer headstart program. *J Spch Hrng Disords, 33:*121-26, 1968.

Morley, Muriel: *Development and Disorders of Speech in Childhood.* London, Livingstone Ltd., 1965.

Mowrer, O. H.: *Language Learning and the Symbolic Processes.* New York, Wiley, 1960.

Mowrer, O. H.: Hearing and speaking: an analysis of language learning. *J Spch Hrng. Disords, 23:*143-152, 1958.

——— Speech development in the young child: I-The autism theory of speech development and some clinical applications. *J Spch Hrng Disords, 17:*263-68, 1952.

——— *Learning Theory and Personality Dynamics.* New York, Ronald Press, 1950.

Myklebust, Helmer: Babbling and echolalia in language theory. *J Spch Hrng Disords, 22:*356-60, 1951.

Mysak, E. *Speech Pathology and Feedback Theory.* Springfield, Thomas, 1966.

——— Organismic development of oral language. *J Spch Hrng Disords 26:* 377-84, 1961.

Naremore, Rita: Teacher judgment of children's speech: a factor analytic study of attitudes. *Spch Monogr, 38:*16-26, 1971.

Netter, Frank: *The Nervous System.* Summit, N. J., Ciba Collection of Med. Illus., 1962.

O'Donnell, Roy, Griffin, Wm., and Norris, R.: Grammatical structures in the speech of children: a transformational analysis. *J Except Exp Educ, 36:*70-77, 1967.

Olim, E.: Maternal language styles and cognitive development of children. In Fredrick Williams (Ed.): *Language and Poverty: Perspectives on a Theme.* Inst. for Res. on Pov. Monogr. Ser. Chicago, Markham Pub. Company, 1970, 212-28.

Orgel, A., and Dreger, R.: A comparative study of the Arthur-Leiter and the Stanford-Binet Intelligence Scales. *J Genet Psychol, 86:*359-65, 1955.

Osborn, S.: Concepts of speech development. *J Spch Hrng Disords, 26:* 391-92, 1955.

Osgood, C., and Miron, M.: *Approaches to the Study of Aphasia.* Urbana, Ill., Univ. of Ill. Press, 1963.

Pei, Mario: *Whats in a Word.* New York, Hawthorn Books, 1968.

——— *The Many Hues of English.* New York, Knopf Pub. Co., 1967.

Peise, W.: Hughlings Jackson's doctrine of aphasia and its significance today. *J Nerv Ment Dis. 122:*1-13, 1955.

Penfield, Wilder: The uncommitted cortex: the child's changing brain. *Atlantic Monthly, 214:*77-81, July 1964.

Penfield, Wilder, and Roberts, L.: *Speech and Brain Mechanism.* Princeton, N. J., Princeton Univ. Press, 1959.

Penfield, Wilder, and Rasmussen, T.: *The Cerebral Cortex of Man.* New York, McMillan, 1950.

Piaget, Jean: *Six Psychological Studies.* New York, Random House, 1967.

——— *The Language and Thought of the Child.* London, Routledge, 1959.

——— *Development of Reality in the Child.* New York, Basic Books, 1954.

——— Communication Between Children. In Wayne Dennis (Ed.): *Readings in Child Psychology.* Englewood Cliffs, N. J., Prentice Hall, 1963, 211-215.

Ponder, E.: Understanding the language of the culturally disadvantaged child. *Elem English, 42:*769-74, 1965.

Poussaint, Alvin F.: Why Blacks kill Blacks. *Ebony,* 62-64, October 1970.

Ravens, J. C.: *Guide to Using the Coloured Progressive Matrices (Sets A, Ab, B).* London, H. K. Lewis, 1960.

Riley, J. E.: *The Influence of Bilingualism on Tested Verbal Ability in Spanish and English: Final Report* (microfilm). Denton, Texas, Texas Women's Univ., 1968, 24 pp.

Robbins, Samuel, and Robbins, Rosa S.: *Speech Sound Discrimination and Verbal Imagery Type Test.* Magnolia, Mass., Expression Co., 1966.

Sanford, Fillmore, and Wrightsman, L.: Language development. In *Psychology: A Scientific Study of Man.* Belmont, Calif., Brooks/Cole Pub. Co., 1970, 78-88.

Sapir, E.: *Language.* New York, Harcourt Brace and World, 1921.

Saporta, Sol: *Psycholinguistics: A Book of Readings.* New York, Holt Rinehart and Winston, 1961.

Saunders, R., and Norsinger, R.: Structure and lexicon in sentence processing. *Spch Monogr, 38:*27-34, 1971.

Saunders, William: *The Larynx.* Summit, N. J., Ciba Collection of Med. Illus., 1964.

Schoenfeld, W. H., and Keller, F. S.: *Principles of Psychology: A Schematic Text in the Science of Behavior.* New York, Appleton Century Crofts, 1950.

Sekyra, F., and Arnoult, J.: Negro intellectual assessment with three instruments contrasting Caucasian and Negro norms. *J Learn Disabils, 1:*564-69, 1968.

Shriner, T. H., and Miner, L.: Morphological structures in the language of the disadvantaged and advantaged. *J Spch Hear Res, 11:*605-10, 1968.

Shuy, R.: The sociolinguists and urban language problems. In Fredrick Williams (Ed.): *Language and Poverty: Perspectives on a Theme.* Inst. Res. Pov. Monogr. Ser. Chicago, Markham Pub. Co., 1970, 335-50.

Sigel, I., and Perry, C.: Psycholinguistic diversity among culturally deprived children. *Amer J Orthopsychiat, 38:*122-27, 1968.

Sinclair-deZwart, H.: Developmental psycholinguistics. In D. Elkind and J. Flavell (Eds.): *Studies in Cognitive Development: Essays in Honor of Jean Piaget.* New York, Oxford Univ. Press, 1969, 315-36.

Skinner, F. F.: *Verbal Behavior.* New York, Appleton Century Crofts, 1957.

Sloan, W.: *The Lincoln-Oseretsky Motor Development Scale.* Los Angeles, West. Psychol. Serv., 1955.

Slobin, D. I.: Comments on developmental psycholinguistics. In F. A. Smith and G. Miller (Eds.): *The Genesis of Language: A Psycholinguistic Approach.* Cambridge, Mass., MIT Press, 1966, 85-92.

——— Grammatical transformations and sentence comprehension in childhood and adulthood. *J Verb Learn Verb Behav, 5:*219-27, 1966.

Smith, Alfred (Ed.): *Communication and Culture.* New York, Holt Rinehart and Winston, 1966.

Smith, C.: An experimental approach to children's linguistic competence. In John Hayes (Ed.): *Cognition and the Development of Language.* New York, John Wiley and Sons, 1970, 109-33.

Smith, F., and Miller, G. (Eds.): *The Genesis of Language: A Psycholinguistic Approach.* Cambridge, Mass., MIT Press, 1966.

Smith, Riley B.: Interrelatedness of certain deviant grammatical structures in negro non-standard dialects. *J Engl Linguistics, 3*:82-88, 1968.

Staats, A. W.: *Language Learning and Cognition.* New York, Holt Rinehart and Winston, 1968.

Stewart, William: Urban Negro speech: sociolinguistic factors affecting English teaching. In R. Shuy (Ed.): *Social Dialects and Language Learning.* Champaign, Ill., NCTE, 1965.

——— Toward a history of American Negro dialect. In Fredrick Williams (Ed.): *Language and Poverty: Perspectives on a Theme.* Instit. Res. Pov. Monogr. Ser. Chicago, Markham Pub. Co., 1970, 351-79.

Stone, Lawrence and Church, Joseph: Stages in learning language. In *Childhood and Adolescence.* New York, Random House, 1957, 232-46.

Strauss, A., and Kephart, N.: *Psychopathology and Education of the Brain Injured Child: Vol. II.* New York, Grune and Stratton, 1955.

Stutsman, Rachael: *Mental Measurement of Preschool Children.* New York, World Book Company, 1931.

Subcommittee on Human Communication and its Disorders (National Advisory Neurological Diseases and Stroke Council). *Human Communication and its Disorders: An Overview.* Bethesda, Md., U.S. Dept. of HEW, Natl. Instit. of Health, Pub. Health Serv., 1969.

Sugar, Oscar: Congenital aphasia: an anatomical and physiological approach. *J Spch Hrng Disords, 17*:301-04, 1952.

Templin, Mildred: *Certain Language Skills in Children.* Instit. Child Welf. Monogr. Ser. #26, Minneapolis, Univ. of Minn. Press, 1957.

——— Speech development in the young child: III, the development of certain language skills in children. *J Spch Hrng Disords, 17*:280-85, 1952.

Templin, Mildred and Darley, F.: *The Templin-Darley Tests of Articulation.* Iowa City, Bur. Educa. Res., State Univ. of Iowa, 1960.

Terman, L., and Merrill, M.: *Measuring Intelligence.* New York, Houghton Mifflin, 1937.

Travis, Lee (Ed.): *Handbook of Speech Pathology.* New York, Appleton Century Crofts, 1957.

Trevino, Bertha: Bilingual instructions in the primary grades. *Mod Lang J, 4*:255-56, 1970.

Turner, L.: *Africanism in the Gullah Dialect.* Chicago, Univ. of Chicago Press, 1949.

Van Riper, Charles: *Speech Correction, Principles and Practices.* Englewood Cliffs, N. J., Prentice Hall, 1963.

Vetter, Harold: *Language Behavior and Communication.* Itasca, Ill., S. E. Peacock, 1969.

Vygotsky, L. S.: *Thought and Language.* Cambridge, Mass., MIT Press, 1962.

Waisman, R.: In defense of new and uncommon uses of language. In

Patrick Gleason and Nancy Wakefield (Eds.): *Language and Culture.* Columbus, Ohio, C. E. Merrill, 1968, 135-150.

Wakefield, N. W., and Silvarali, N. S.: A study of oral language patterns of low socio-economic groups. *Reading Teacher, 22*:622-24, 1962.

Wechsler, David: *Wechsler Scales of Preschool and Primary Intelligence.* New York, Psychol. Corp., 1949.

——— *Wechsler Intelligence Scale for Children.* New York, Psychol. Corp., 1949.

Weisenberg, T., and McBride, K.: *Aphasia.* New York, Commonwealth Fund, 1935.

Wepman, Joseph, Jones, L., Brock, R., and Van Pelt, D.: Studies in aphasia: background and theoretical information. *J Spch Hrng Disords, 25*:323-332, 1960.

West, Robert, and Ansberry, M.: *The Rehabilitation of Speech.* New York, Harper and Row, 1968.

Whipp, Leslie: The child as language teacher. *Elem English, 46*:466-70, 1969.

White, B.: The initial coordination of sensori-motor schemas in human infants-Piaget's ideas and the role of experience. In D. Elkind and J. Flavell (Eds.): *Studies in Cognitive Development: Essays in Honor of Jean Piaget.* New York, Oxford Univ. Press, 1969, 237-56.

Whorf, Benjamin Lee: *Language, Thought and Reality.* Cambridge, Mass., John Wiley, 1956.

Willard, L. A.: A comparison of culture fair test scores with group and individual intelligence test scores of disadvantaged Negro children. *J Learn Disabils, 1*:584-89, 1968.

Williams, Cratis: Mountain speech. In Patrick Gleason and Nancy Wakefield (Eds.): *Language and Culture.* Columbus, Ohio, C. E. Merrill, 1968, 151-60.

Williams, F.: Language, attitude, and social change. In F. Williams (Ed.): *Language and Poverty: Perspectives on a Theme.* Instit. Res. on Pov. Monogr. Ser. Chicago, Markham Pub. Co., 1970, 380-99.

——— Psychological correlates of speech characteristics on sounding disadvantaged. *J Spch Hear Res, 13*:472-88, 1971.

Williams, F., and Naremore, R.: Social class differences in children's syntactic performance: a quantitative analysis of field study data. *J Spch Hear Res, 12*:778-93, 1969.

Williams, John and Edwards, C. Drew: An exploratory study of the modification of color and racial concept attitudes in preschool children. *Child Dev, 40*:727-736, 1969.

Winitz, H.: Repetitions in the vocalizations and speech of children in the first two years of life. *J Spch Hrng Disords, Monogr. Suppl. #7*, 55-62, 1961.

Wolfram, W.: Sociolinguistic premises and the nature of nonstandard dialects. *Elem. English, 47*:739-48, 1970.

Wood, Barbara and Curry, J.: Everyday TALK and school TALK of the city Black child. *Spch Teacher, 18*:282-96, 1969.

Woodburne, Lloyd: *The Neural Basis of Behavior*. Columbus, Ohio, C. E. Merrill, 1967.

Worley, S., and Stony, W.: Socio-economic status and language facility of the beginning first graders. *Reading Teacher, 20*:400-03, 1967.

Zemlin, Willard: *Speech and Hearing Science: Anatomy and Physiology*. Englewood Cliffs, N. J., Prentice Hall, 1968.

APPENDIX

Suggested Discussion Questions

A. 1. Develop what, in your opinion, would be an adequate definition for "abstraction" as related to language functions.
2. Differentiate speech and language.
3. What is the role of perception in the development of language as a coding system of cultural values?
4. Explain the nature of social interaction in the development of attitudinal sets.
5. Describe the link between conceptualization and attitudinal sets.
6. How does our perception of the listener cloud our view of the communication process?
7. What, in your opinion, is a feasible theory of the origin of language in man?

B. 1. How is propositional speech related to self-image?
2. What does the complexity of language suggest in regard to the nature-nuture theory of language development; i.e. species-specific versus conditioned-reinforced theories?
3. What can we assume about the carry-over of taste-testing experiences to speech sound development and proprioception?
4. How does vocalization vary when a six-month-old infant is alone and when his mother is with him?
5. Differentiate egocentric speech and socialized speech.
6. How is intellectual growth related to psycho-social adaptive skills?
7. Differentiate the concept of development and the concept of intelligence.
8. What are the four major requirements for language?
9. How is babbling behavior related to language development?

C. 1. How is syntagmatic sound development related to articulation proficiency?
2. What is the function of pivot words in the early stages of language development?
3. Does environment alter the variety and complexity of language learning?
4. Discuss the nature and complexity of phonology in terms of the competence-performance dichotomy.
5. How is the development of morphemes related to syntactic development?
6. Explain the function of single word utterances in the first stages of verbal behavior.

7. Describe two experiences that an infant might have in his normal daily routine that would tend to aid in the development of downward categorization.
8. Discuss two theories that explain why a child uses more concrete rather than abstract terms.

D. 1. How are reflex patterns related to speech sound production?
2. Trace motor control in reach-grasp manipulation in the early stages of motor development.
3. What is the link between neurological maturation and multilingual skills?
4. What is the role of the Central Nervous System in language development?
5. Why is cortico-thalamic function important in the study of neurological organization?

E. 1. Which of the theories of cognitive development stress the importance of reinforcement?
2. How are school experiences related to categorization and cognitive functions?
3. What are the three major stages of cognitive development as described in the servomechanism approach to language learning.
4. How does the Piagetian approach describe the link between perception and cognition?
5. Identify an incident which would tend to help the child develop skills in problem solving.

F. 1. How does comprehension and extension contribute to cognitive development?
2. Summarize the transition from the period of syncretism to phenomenalism.
3. Discuss the relationship of time concepts and the development of "When . . ." and "What for . . ." questions.
4. Specify the type of play activities that would demonstrate egocentric behaviors as opposed to socialized behaviors.
5. What psycho-social behaviors are typical of a three-year-old?
6. How does Bruner describe stages of eye-hand coordination and adaptive behavior in infants?
7. How is role playing related to risk-free experimentation?

G. 1. Differentiate the deficit theory and the difference theory of dialect language patterns.
2. Identify possible reasons for similarities and differences in speech patterns in children from different social structures.
3. Differentiate an observation of lower socioeconomic family styles as it might be reported by deficit theorists and the descriptive linguists approach.
4. How can transformational grammar be utilized in the study of dialect differences?

5. Differentiate plurality as evidenced in standard and dialect language samples.
6. Which of the language development theories of dialect differences appear to be based on stimulus-bound theories of language aquisiition? Which of the theories appear to incorporate the idea of language universals?

H. 1. Describe two tests of intelligence: one involving speed and one involving power.
2. Is it possible to expect that a child might be able to perform better on one type of test than on another? If so, why? Would language differences account for performance differences?
3. Describe a method of evaluating language skills that will minimize cultural differences.
4. Differentiate verbal and non-verbal test instruments. How can non-verbal test measures be effectively used in the evaluation of language skills?

NAME INDEX

SUBJECT INDEX